STRENGTH OF A WOMAN

... The Truth About Training The Female Body

By Roger Schwab

MAIN
LINE
PUBLICATIONS

Copyright © 1997 Main Line Publications

First Printing June 1997

Second Printing November 1997, revised

All Rights Reserved.
Reproduction of any portion of this book in any form or by any means, except for appropriate use in critical reviews, is forbidden without the written permission of the publisher.

Cover Design: Todd Davidson

Layout and Design: Todd Davidson

Cover Photo: Kris Eckenrode

Photography: Kris Eckenrode

Editor: Elanna Schwab

Library of Congress Catalog Card Number: 97-93279

ISBN: 0-9656490-0-8

MAIN
LINE
PUBLICATIONS

931 Haverford Road • Bryn Mawr, PA 19010

Toll Free: 1-888-97WOMAN

Printed in the United States of America

To those women who look past the infomercials, compromises and total sell-outs. To those who seek the truth and realize that the only bargain is quality.

"Somewhere beyond the barricade is there a world you long to see?"

— *"Do You Hear The People Sing?"*
Les Miserables

STRENGTH OF A WOMAN

... The Truth About Training The Female Body

By Roger Schwab

CONTENTS

I. Warm-Up
    About The Author..ix
    Preface..x
    Strong Words.. xiii

II. The Truth
    1. The Aerobic Fallacy..1
    2. One-Stop Shopping... 12
    3. Time is Precious... 19
    4. Function is Everything... 27
    5. Bodybuilding: Myths and Missteps..................... 51
    6. The Right Track..58
    7. Psychological Roadblocks.................................... 66
    8. Battling Nature... 73
    9. Rehabilitation... 89

III. The Workout
    10. Principles... 95
    11. Sample Workouts.. 110

IV. Cool Down
    A Final Word.. 157
    Acknowledgements... 158
    Index..159

About The Author

Roger Schwab, born in Philadelphia on April 6, 1945, resides in Bryn Mawr, the heart of Philadelphia's Main Line. An author, poet, teacher of sports/medicine, Schwab's many interests focus primarily on political science, music, and health and fitness related issues. A product of the 60's, Schwab's major influences include the writings of Gore Vidal, David Halberstam and Norman Mailer. His musical tastes are defined by the lyrics and music of Bob Dylan, Leonard Cohen, Joan Baez and the late Phil Ochs and Buddy Holly. Schwab's passionate involvement with meaningful exercise was cultivated to foundation through the writing and acquaintance of Arthur Jones.

Preface

I have spent an exorbitant amount of time in thought about the field of exercise and specifically the aspect of strength training.

A lifelong passion, strength training and its boundaries have risen in my life from a post pubescent interest to a full time business interest, complete with a full lecturing schedule, newspaper columns, professional physique adjudicating as well as owning and operating a 25,000 square foot state of the art fitness and sports medicine complex and osteoporosis diagnostic testing center in the academically fertile climate of Bryn Mawr, PA in the heart of Philadelphia's Main Line.

In the early 1960's, mainly due to the fact that people interested in any form of weight training were looked upon as either "weirdoes" or of "no class", sensible information on this chosen subject was at best sparse (and please note, the key word here is sensible and in that respect, little has changed over the past 30 some odd years), I struck out on my own, asking questions along the way, usually to those who looked the best and usually knew the least. Arthur Jones, Nautilus founder and my sole major influence on the subject, later said in the early 1970's - "there is generally an inverse relationship between the size of the biceps and the function of the brain," - words that would have been of great benefit to me in my early years in sifting out fact from fraud and fiction in the strength training community. I always prided myself on being a good listener and usually proceeded to experiment on myself the training routines preached by others in my direction. Some worked, most did not as I quietly worked my way up the ladder in a sport which I dared not broach to my family and which participation in (weightlifting) was deemed narcissistic at best and appealing to one's lowest instincts. I was thus hesitant to destroy any credibility my otherwise studious mind may have created.

My academic career at Penn State was highlighted by a brief stint as the first unofficial strength coach beginning in the Fall of 1963. A position acquired, not from degrees behind my name, but by a victory in the first Pennsylvania State Powerlifting Championships and a lean, mean (albeit usually injured) physique to go with it. Putting into practice what I had gleaned from the area "experts" left a lot to be desired during my tenure. Of relevance, however, was a discovery that I learned about myself at this crucial growth (as in intellectual growth) stage. I found through trial and error, that I not only experienced what I saw around myself, but I learned from those experiences. It quickly came to my attention that I should not take that fact for granted. Some people merely experience life's surroundings while others experience and learn. The former seemed destined to repeat their mistakes, literally on a "treadmill to nowhere."

Through on the job training, (an extremely effective way to learn), I found myself able to somewhat accurately differentiate fact from opinion. This helped immeasurably through the years. I learned in the field of strength training that common sense was anything but common. This observation applied to many published experts and schooled scholars who should know better. Everyone has opinions and we are all entitled to one, but that does not mean all opinions are of equal value. Basic physics is not subject to opinion.

I have ventured in many different directions in the field of strength training to this time, more than most, I would guess. I have seen the "inner sanctum" of the physique world as an international judge. I have lectured to medical doctors, trainers, teachers, women's groups and nearly anyone whose stipulation was information on safe, sensible exercise.

This book is a result of my road to understanding on a topic misunderstood by most. A topic which, if understood, will highly elevate the quality of life of literally anyone who undertakes it. Far from being the narcissistic endeavor as viewed by yesterday's ignorance and today's uninformed, the meaningful principles put forth in this book might well be the most important physiological ideals ever presented to the women of the Twenty First Century. Although this book epitomizes female strength training, the same principles and philosophy can be applied to male strength training.

Strength Of A Woman tells the truth about safe, sensible strength training for females. It is not an exercise physiology textbook, nor is it based on documented "strength" studies – most of which have been based on equipment incapable of truly measuring strength development. Rather, this book reflects empirical evidence and common sense.

I have no financial involvement with the equipment manufacturers mentioned in this book. I do have, however, a stake in meaningful exercise, and a desire to identify what is right and wrong with the industry – even if my perspective bucks the tide. In a real sense, this is a personal statement ... and it is an informed one.

– Roger Schwab

Strong Words

The fitness field is ruled by charlatans. They're not after your body – they want your wallet. The past two decades have seen an explosion of gyms, equipment, gadgetry, videos, books, booklets and bombast. Professional athletes, fashion models, bodybuilders, and other self-styled prophets of health all claim to have the workout that works. Ranging from innocuous stretching and tummy twisting (for women) to brutal, take-no-prisoners regimens of heaving iron (for men), popular programs are craftily conceived but usually devoid of merit. They constitute a marketplace of misinformation. And no one is getting "ripped off" worse than women.

Nobody's telling the truth because the truth doesn't sell. It doesn't sell in print, on video, or in the gym. Self-appointed fitness gurus treat women not just as a separate gender, but as a different species. Tough training is out; powder puff is in.

Browse in the Health & Fitness section of your local bookstore. There is no shortage of material. There is, however, a paucity of sensible advice. Books about weight training and bodybuilding for men fairly clang with the sound of thumping barbells and bulging muscles. We're talking serious poundage, vicious workouts, animal rage, massive muscularity and – for the average practitioner – a pipe dream.

Now check the women's shelf. Book after book describes fluffy exercises that purport to "tone" the body. ("Lie on your side and lift .... bend over and twist your trunk," etc., etc.) Photographs show smiling, shapely women clutching small, light, gleaming dumbbells and demonstrating various movements that will, presumably, endow your body with a new set of curves.

Not on this planet. Those pictures are a lie. The model didn't get that way simply by twisting and stretching and twirling hand weights of polished steel. Either genetics, cosmetic surgery, or far more rigorous training produced the figure you see in the photographs.

Mass appeal often strays from the truth. For the truth, you must look beyond the magazine racks and the video shelves that reflect the desire for muscular profits rather than a stronger, firmer populace. The book that you hold in your hands is a good place to start. And as far as the truth is concerned, you need go no further.

In discovering the truth, you will find irony. For instance, you'll learn that more rigorous does not mean more time-consuming. In fact, the program that is most effective for women takes less time than the slew of ineffectual routines detailed on videotape and between book covers. But while you're at work, you must work hard. You must be willing to push your throttle to the max for relatively short periods of time. That is where overall fitness lies.

In the wayward world of physical conditioning – where experts are quickly anointed once they win a contest or make a beauty commercial – women were first ignored, then duped. The notion of segregated training persists, as old-school thinkers still see men straining in dungeon-type facilities, while women are consigned to pretty-in-pink; men lifting heavy weights (with little consideration given to form), women harnessed to ridiculous contraptions vibrating around their hips.

My philosophy has always been to train people as people, to train men and women together on the same equipment in the same environment, and not regard women as weaklings and men as barbarians. Remarkably, on a national level, this philosophy has captured few converts. In the avalanche of books and tapes, we find women doing meaningless, mindless exercises. We see men whose Herculean muscles – often pharmaceutically enhanced – pull titanic weight. Depending on your perception, it's either a fantasy or a nightmare.

Be aware that there's a middle ground where 99 percent of us can find secure footing. What has always worked – and always will work – for people of any age is safe, meaningful, intelligent resistance training. This book will explain why that is so, and describe the path to the solid middle ground.

The Truth
1. The Aerobic Fallacy

Joint stress accumulates silently.

In the late 1960's and early 1970's, Dallas-based physician Dr. Kenneth Cooper pioneered the premise that aerobic training improves the functioning of the heart and lungs, and in so doing creates a more vibrant individual.

There is truth in that. Aerobic exercise elevates the heart rate to X level for Y period of time with Z results. When practiced regularly, it improves cardio-respiratory efficiency. Though a lower resting heart rate doesn't

Aerobic classes often apply "Madison Avenue" clichés in order to attract customers. Workouts with catchy titles such as "Body Sculpting," "Butt Blasting" and "Thigh Slimming" cannot accomplish any of their intended functions. Meaningful long term results are derived from safe, structured strength training exercises.

No Truth

How well I remember first meeting a "lean and mean" young actress on the East Coast via Los Angeles. It was the early 1970's in New York City at a well known "training institute". In a word, she looked great. Tight and toned with no "excess baggage", she was belted into one of the old Nautilus pullover-type torso machines, which was enhanced with additional seat and back pads so that she would fit in the machine correctly. No matter, she was training hard, and she never quit! Every exercise was taken to the point of "failure". When she finished her workout non-stop, machine to machine, she was beat. It was also obvious that she felt great about her workout and herself! Her presence totally filled the room.

I remember the down I felt when her first workout video was released a short time later. No machines, no training to failure, no "eye of the tiger" look. And no truth.

guarantee longer life (although it seemingly might), it does mean that the body has more stamina however long it lasts.

The benefits of aerobics are obvious, and canny marketers have been quick to take advantage of its appeal: movement, music, a non-threatening way to shape up. But for all of its benefits, aerobics has limitations. It does not completely enhance the structural integrity of the connective tissues, the joints, and the bones themselves. (Indeed, it often tests them to the breaking point). It does not appreciably strengthen the muscles. It does not and cannot make the body *firmer.*

Yet the message conveyed by hugely popular videotapes is just that. The suggestion, the implication – even the claim – is that the aerobic workout will transform you into a facsimile of the group leader. But aerobics alone will not make you look like Jane or Cindy or Cathy or whomever, no matter how much you step, hop, twist, and sweat.

Step aerobic classes gained popularity after the introduction and commercial success of stairclimbing machines. Both exercises may potentially stimulate cardiovascular benefits, however, neither will substantially firm the hip or thigh muscles nor strengthen the bones. A far better choice for realizing physiological or aesthetic goals is to follow the strength training program outlined in this book.

The image, however, is seductive, and aerobics has become a buzzword for total fitness. Even the American College of Sports Medicine (a professional organization consisting of educators, physicians, and exercise physiologists) has until recently regarded aerobics as virtually a complete exercise program. An entire generation has been reared to the beat, puppets in thrall to the video masters. Exercisers impart strength-building qualities to stationary cycles, cross-country skiing machines, walking with hand weights, steppers, treadmills, and other aerobic equipment, but in reality, strength gains are insignificant.

Society has been bamboozled. The very nature of aerobic exercise makes it impossible to realize the meaningful strength gains necessary for a noticeable improvement in muscle tone. Burn calories, yes; strengthen muscle, no. When you are working aerobically (i.e. brisk walking), your muscles work against minimal or zero resistance and, therefore, can continue to function at the same level for a long period of time. This is not the route to building strength, and only strength creates muscular shape and stronger bones – the aesthetics that are prized, and the foundation needed for the long haul. Aerobic exercise improves general functioning via a potentially lower heart rate (greater heart-lung efficiency), but it does not strengthen the muscles around the joints (thus enhancing joint stability) and it does not substantially strengthen or firm the body.

What is missing from the equation is serious strength training. Because the truth is you can work your heart/lungs and muscles/bones in the same safe, sound workout. Visualize a muscle as a mass of individual fibers. Aerobic exercise requires that only a small number of available muscle fibers contract over a long period of time. It takes an intense contraction of the muscle to utilize many more of its fibers and stimulate meaningful strength gain. This type of exercise, *anaerobic* exercise, induces fatigue in the muscle faster than the muscle can compensate. Working against sufficient resistance, the muscle fatigues quickly, and the individual soon is unable to perform the exercise at that level of resistance. This is the principle of working the muscle to the point of momentary muscular "failure" (the inability to complete another repetition in perfect form), and it is the ticket to gaining strength. Such exercise stimulates the overall system to respond. Rest permits that response.

It may sound grim, this whole notion of failure and resistance, as opposed to a high-decibel aerobics class. But it is the one true way to strengthen the body.

> *MYTH: Aerobic training makes the body firmer.*
>
> *FACT: It takes stronger muscles to produce a firmer body, and only anaerobic exercise - working against sufficient resistance - will meaningfully strengthen the muscles.*

Still, the allure of aerobics as a supposed full-body, all-purpose workout persists. After all, the arms and the legs are in motion, sweat is flying, calories are burning, fat is dissolving, the music is pulsating, and women figure, yes, this is the way to get in shape. And indeed, improved cardiovascular functioning is an important part of being in shape. But less body fat and improved wind do not mean a stronger, harder, more durable body. The only way to make the body firmer is to get stronger, and the only way to get stronger is to be progressive with your exercise. Aerobic exercising – whether on an open floor, a stair-climber, a bicycle, a treadmill, or a track – does not provide the progressive resistance necessary to develop meaningful strength. It is not designed to work the muscles throughout their full range-of-motion. Yes, a strong heart and efficient lungs are an important part of what the body needs to function at an optimum level and ward off long-range debilitating conditions. However, aerobic exercise is not the whole story.

A woman who is out of shape and takes up aerobics may notice some physiological changes in her body initially, but this will quickly level off because she is not seriously challenging her starting strength level. The same phenomenon occurs if she begins a weightlifting program and uses extremely light dumbbells. Curling, say, a 2-pound weight 100 times may make her breathe hard, perspire handily, and ache, but it does not stimulate the biceps muscle to get measurably stronger and, thus, firmer. This becomes, essentially, an aerobic exercise.

However, if the same woman trains progressively and reaches a point where she can curl 50 pounds 10 times, she has been working deeper into her starting strength level and has given a wakeup call to all those muscle fibers that were lying dormant. She has gained strength, and the shape of her body will show it. Please be assured that our goal is not to heave heavy weights, and the results are not bulging muscles – results that are beyond the reach of almost all women, anyway. Our goal is to develop a lean, strong, healthy, toned body. Building muscle size is extremely difficult for most men who have the potential to do so, let alone women who don't want them in the first place.

Stressed-out Joints

Now that you understand what aerobic exercise can and cannot accomplish, consider a potential problem that may arise for the enthusiastic runner, jogger, or aerobic dancer. When performed over a stretch of an individual's lifetime, repetitive pounding movements may have a telling cost. Joint stress, you see, accumulates silently.

When I was younger, I competed in cross-country races and covered many rocky, hilly miles on a weekly basis. When I turned 40, though I had not done any serious running for years, I started experiencing pain in my lower back and down my legs. I did not equate that pain with running my heart out as a kid, yet it was the direct, if delayed, result of my excessive running 20 years earlier along with my serious misuse of a barbell.

Doctors call this the "overuse" syndrome, and it can take you by surprise. One day you get sudden aches and pains – not traceable to what you did yesterday, but to the sins of your past. (Of course, the same symptoms can be triggered by a recent trauma and may, or may not, be linked to old habits.) What has occurred here is that the cumulative effect of impact force has exceeded the structural integrity of bone, muscle, and connective tissue. The certain result: injury. High impact exercises take their toll on vulnerable bones, joints and tissue.

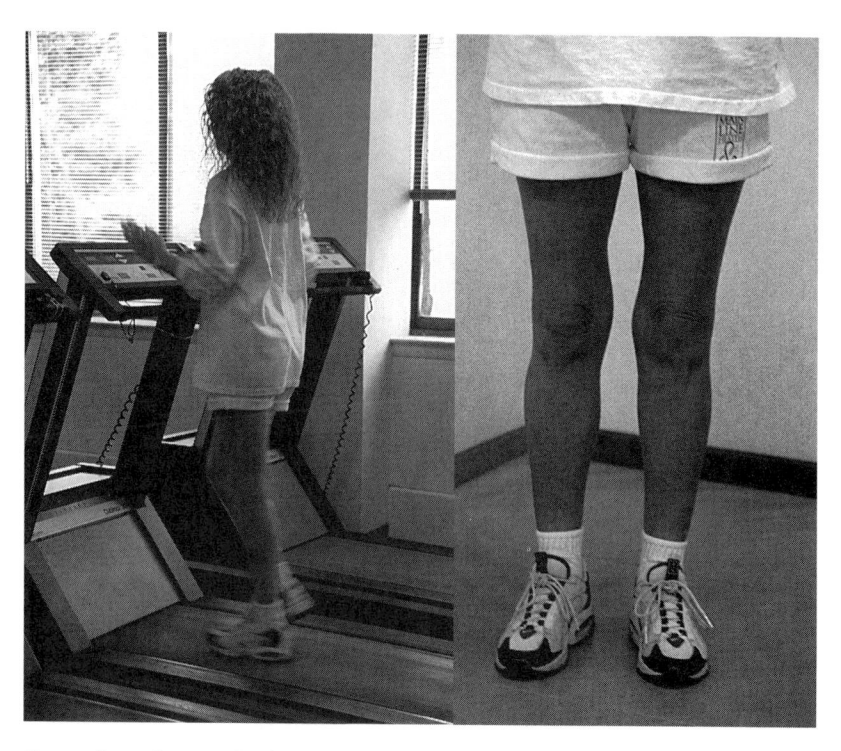

Running through the years does little to strengthen muscles above the knee (vastus medialis), essential to protecting the vulnerable, inefficient knee joint.

Too Much

Though it is rarely stated in print, empirical evidence suggests that too much exercise can actually hasten degenerative change, over time wearing down the musculoskeletal system. Continuous, repetitive movement may cause friction in the joints and culminate in a painful range of movement and an altering of body mechanics. Trouble can even come from unlikely sources. Stationary bicycle riding, for example, is usually considered a safe exercise since pedaling produces horizontal movement which eliminates most of the inherent impact forces associated with jogging. However, excessive use over time can potentially wear down an inefficient knee or hip. This problem, like many problems associated with exercise, can be prevented by understanding the cause and effect of exercise reiterated constantly throughout this book. Properly performed exercise stimulates a response from the overall system, rest allows that response.

Pounding on hard surfaces and repetitive movement creates such an impact - which problem is accelerated when there is not strong muscle surrounding the joints.

One lesson learned from all this is that, instead of a tremendous amount of exercise, we should seek the least amount to stimulate the maximum result. I have constantly searched for ways to shorten exercise periods – without compromising the results – in order to avoid overusing the muscles, exhausting the system, and overtaxing the joints. When the route to high cardiovascular fitness entails pounding the pavement for 10, 15, 20 miles a week, the risk of muscular injury, bone and joint damage, and strained tendons and ligaments rises. The most susceptible areas are the knee, foot, ankle, lower back, hip and cervical spine. Is this high level of conditioning worth the cost? When you find yourself on the shelf, you may not think so. Furthermore, your fine-tuned condition will slip as you sit on the sidelines for long extended periods, or during recurrent episodes of nagging injuries.

This fate can be avoided and top condition still attained via high intensity circuit-type strength training, for this kind of program should involve no orthopedic cost, no damage to the skeleton.

Proper exercise should strengthen the muscles, connective tissues and bones. It should never damage the skeleton. Improving your cardiovascular condition at a high orthopedic risk does not make sense for most people. There is a safer, more sensible way to go about the quest for well-rounded fitness, a short direct route to improving your cardiovascular condition and strengthening your muscles and bones at the same time while minimizing the risk of injury.

Sometimes, aerobic enthusiasts who are fanatical about their workouts will eventually run right into problems. Some can't seem to get enough of the so-called "runners high" – that feeling of well-being that arises when compounds known as endorphins are released in the body and interact with the brain. But in the quest of great mileage and realizing ultimate aerobic benefit – it may be at an orthopedic cost.

I don't believe there is such a thing as super health. I do believe, however, in *good* health, and there is no question that efficient cardiovascular functioning promotes vitality. If for example, you like to run, fine – not overdone, it can be good exercise. Just know why you are doing it, and don't overdo it, because the excessive pounding carries the long-term risk in many individuals of creating major joint injury. And realize that neither excessive running nor other popular forms of aerobic exercise will safely strengthen your muscles, safely strengthen your bones, or shape your body.

Danger Zone: More is not better

There are greater dangers associated with excess. Too much aerobic exercising may go beyond the burning of fat, and burn lean muscle tissue: something like overdosing on certain vitamins to the point where they become toxic to the body. For women in particular, this path can be quite distressing. Excessive aerobic exercise in combination with very low body fat levels may lead to an interrupted monthly menstrual cycle and the onset of premature bone loss. The conditions of anorexia and bulimia can also be associated with such compulsive behavior.

That's the drastic end of the scale, but useful for everyone to keep in mind. Most women avoid these traps, but are still inclined to believe that aerobic exercise provides a full body workout, and that more exercise automatically pays greater dividends. Those assumptions do not hold up, because more is quite often not better, and aerobic conditioning – no matter how strenuous – does not forge taut, toned bodies.

The majority of women begin an exercise program with the sincere desire to lose weight. Many of them are willing to do almost any amount of exercise to achieve that goal.

Balanced Diet

Breakfast – Shredded Wheat with fruit and whole grain toast.

Lunch – Low fat turkey sandwich with fruit.

Dinner – Fish, skinless chicken or lean meat with a vegetable, salad, and/or a baked potato.

These meals are the staples of a balanced, well-rounded diet and serve only as an example of the quantity and quality of food which is recommended by the National Research Council.

Note: Drink water continuously throughout the day. Liquid staples such as low-fat or skim milk and/or citrus juices may also be consumed during meals.

Alas, exercise is not the most efficient way to burn body fat. The most efficient and sensible way to lose weight is to eat less food. Eating small portions of a well-balanced diet (as recommended by the National Research Council) comprised of a variety of foods will work for virtually everyone. That common-sense approach, however, is not popular. The sensible combination of training hard (though briefly) and eating less has always been the sound way to a lean, hard body. But many women feel that, if they exercise more (usually much more), they can eat freely and still lose weight.

The increased exercise is more likely to eventually knock them out of action than to knock off the extra pounds.

2. One-Stop Shopping

Exercising to build strength can also improve stamina – the two need not be separate.

The acceptance of aerobic exercise as a total body workout has been reinforced by another erroneous assumption: weight training makes the muscles stronger but does not improve heart-lung efficiency or burn fat.

It is true that many weight-training regimens, as practiced by newcomers who don't know and veteran lifters who should know better, do not provide the world's greatest cardiovascular workout. This is usually due to the belief that the same muscle group should be worked through several sets of the same exercise. As a result, the lifter needs substantial rest periods between sets, believing his or her muscles need time to refuel. We will see that such pauses are unnecessary in a properly structured, high intensity circuit-type strength workout.

So the conventional wisdom has been that lifting

weights doesn't push the pulse to a high enough level for a continuous period of time to improve cardiovascular fitness. This thinking is evident particularly in the sports world. Coaches and trainers may recognize that aerobic exercise by itself will not adequately strengthen the athlete's muscles, so they construct training programs that are divided into aerobic and anaerobic components. The typical scenario: running to develop stamina, weight training to build strength.

This training regimen gets results, but consider the costs. Compared to a single, high intensity circuit-type strength workout, the twofold program takes more than twice as much time – time that could be put to better use practicing the sports skills involved. Combining roadwork with lifting weights is often double duty, and benefits gained enter the realm of diminishing returns, because as the quantity of exercise increases, intensity decreases.

More importantly, the dual workout heightens the risk of overworking the muscles and joints, and sustaining an injury. The individual becomes exhausted, overtrained, and – pop – something goes. The injury and subsequent inactivity defeat the whole purpose of the training program.

This is true for male or female, athlete or non-athlete.

The fact is that you can work the muscles anaerobically, and simultaneously experience an aerobic effect. All you need to do is elevate your heart rate by working intensely, and moving quickly from exercise to exercise.

This is the most efficient, most orthopedically sound training – the biggest bang for your buck. As I will discuss later, certain weight training machines – as opposed to free weights (barbells, dumbbells) – are the most efficient and orthopedically sound equipment you can use for this purpose.

Remember, where exercise is concerned, more is not better. Look for as little exercise as possible to get the desired result.

VO2 Debate

Since the 1970's in the advent of the "aerobics revolution" aerobic fitness has been equated with overall health with maximal oxygen uptake being the determinate measure of aerobic fitness. Aerobic fitness is essentially the improved ability of the body to extract and utilize oxygen by way of exercise that involves large muscle groups, is rhythmic in nature and can be sustained for an extended period of time. Much of the excitement over aerobic fitness can be attributed to Kenneth H. Cooper, M.D. and the publication of his book, <u>Aerobics</u>. Subsequent to the aerobics boom, public health service initiatives pushed vigorous aerobic exercise as a means of improving "health."

The downside of the aerobics revolution is that the public came to believe that aerobic fitness was the end all towards improving overall health. Vigorous high impact aerobic exercise was appealing to only a select few and with a price – increased risk of orthopedic injury. Those who tried and failed to adhere and those who did not try at all were the winners, at least for preserving joint integrity.

Aerobic fitness is only one component of physical fitness and well-being. Maximum oxygen uptake (VO2 max) reflects an individual's ability to extract and utilize oxygen while performing aerobic exercise (i.e. treadmill/walking, running, cycling, or stepping). Failure of the VO2 to increase linearly with increasing workloads indicates cardiac incompetence or instrument failure. My experience in clinical exercise testing revealed that VO2 max varied between instruments used to measure oxygen uptake. The instruments used to measure VO2 max across manufacturers will yield significantly different results. Who had the right answer? VO2 max for comparative purposes must be looked at via the same test methodology and instrumentation. Does treadmill tolerance testing truly reflect one's functional fitness? Certainly not! As for functional fitness, muscular strength and joint range of motion must also be evaluated as VO2 max is not an absolute determinant of overall fitness.

– Charles J. Bixby M.A. Ed., M.S., A.C.S.M.-E.S.

High-intensity, circuit-type strength training can give you everything you need in the same workout. It is the best way to strengthen the muscles, strengthen the bones, get leaner and harder, increase flexibility, improve stamina and lose weight. All of these objectives are attainable within the scope of a sensible, structured training program that consumes less time and involves less risk of injury than do a host of high-profile muscle magazine programs and aerobics classes that fall short of meeting these goals.

> **Full Range Movement**
>
> My definition is an exercise working a muscle through its full range of function – from a stretched position to a fully contracted position with balanced variable resistance throughout the movement. By nature this must be a single joint exercise where there is no "lock-out" as in a compound movement.

There is, however, a trade-off. If you want to cut your time and maximize your gains, you must be willing to work hard. That sounds reasonable, but working hard has different meanings to different people. If you are new to high-intensity resistance training, you may find that your system balks at first: you become breathless, overheated, even nauseous. With a period of careful "break-in" training of a lower intensity level, those symptoms will recede as you adapt to the demands placed on your body, and you gain strength and muscular/cardiovascular endurance. Keep in mind, though, that if a workout is easy, you can count on little gain. Those who make the most progress are those who push themselves the hardest.

Again, *training hard does not mean training long*. It means working at full throttle for a relatively short period of time. It also does not mean explosive. Slow, full-range movements enable the body to build strength in a safe, efficient manner.

Bent over barbell rowing is capable over time of strengthening the upper body musculature, however, with major limitations. First, the smaller muscles of the arms will fatigue long before the torso. Also, the positioning of the body compromises the lumbar spine.

EXAMPLE: Not a full range of movement.

Using the pullover torso machine, the torso muscles perform the work potentially over 200 degrees of movement without arm musculature involvement. This full range exercise cannot be duplicated with free weight exercises.

EXAMPLE: Full range of movement.

Intensity levels vary, and are often a function of age, training experience, physical condition, and that intangible quality known as motivation. But the woman who cannot muster full intensity for strength training will still realize gains from this type of exercising far better than from anything else, so don't feel that you must be a young, athletic powerhouse to get involved.

Some people insist on doing slow stretches and bending movements or a short, aerobic warm-up on a stair climber or a treadmill prior to their strength training workout. That's fine, though properly performed anaerobic exercises have a built-in warm-up – every repetition of a set of an exercise is a warm-up for the harder repetitions at the end of the set. The aerobic warm-up is not necessary physiologically, but as long as it's not lengthy or draining, it can be viewed as a personal preference. Some women find that a 12-15 minute run immediately after a workout prolongs the "edge" and enhances mental toughness.

For those embarking on a fitness program, expectations may figure prominently. By using the program I recommend – resistance training involving full-range movement around the joints – you may not see overnight change. But you will soon see definite change, and feel increased vitality as you draw additional strength from the knowledge that you are training wisely and gearing your body for the long haul. Make your body all that it can be.

You can do that and not have to engage in a hopelessly detailed menu of workouts, or spend your life in the gym, totally exhausted. You can do it by making a half-hour stop twice a week.

But be prepared to be serious.

Nike says get involved and "just do it." The truth is, get involved, but don't "just do it – do it right."

3. Time Is Precious

Maximum Effort + Minimum Time = Maximum Results

The program that I recommend is not for you if you have a compulsion to hang around a gym all day long. If you are convinced that the watchword more is better applies to exercise as it does to mutual-fund shares, then get ready to change your thinking. If you figure that pushing your body to the limit means long hours and endless exercises, then I have a surprise for you.

Going as hard as you can for as long as you can will yield the same result as keeping a slab of chicken on the grill for two hours instead of 15 minutes: your body will become a cinder. True, you must work hard to achieve optimum results. But you must also work smart. And working smart means working short, as in a short amount of time.

Most of us have a few things to do in our lives other than sweating and straining at the gym. Not that a training session is a horror show, but working out should not be regarded as "fun." Derive your fun from tennis and golf, movies and making love. Training that stimulates results is not recreation.

The beauty of brief training sessions is that lengthy ones are worse than a waste of time – they are counterproductive. Instead of stimulating strength, they exhaust the system.

Empirically, what I have found in training many people over many years is that every time we've made a breakthrough in stimulating results, it's been through a reduction in time spent exercising – not as a result of adding exercises or increasing workout time. We've reduced almost to the point where the next step would be to eliminate training entirely. And that would be one step too many.

> MYTH: *The more time you spend training, the greater your results will be.*
>
> FACT: *Training twice a week produces greater results with less wear and tear on the body.*

This inverse relationship between time and results can be quite dramatic. In 1994, three groups of 10 women each (age range 25-40) participated in a 12-week, circuit-training study under my supervision. None of the women had trained previously – all were "unconditioned."

The respective groups trained once, twice, and three times a week. After a two week break-in period, each exercise was performed to the point of failure. The routine consisted of exercises described in workout #2 later in this book. Each group was then tested at intervals of 4, 8 and 12 weeks on a MedX knee machine, which isolates the quadricep muscles and specifically measures torque. After 4 weeks, the three groups showed comparable increases in strength. Testing at the 8-week juncture revealed that the group training three times a week was leveling off in its strength gains, while the other two groups were improving at a higher rate. After 12 weeks, the 3-times-a-week group, on average, was starting to lose strength, while the other two groups still showed isometric strength gains in the quadriceps muscles (the muscles tested by the machine).

Conclusion: the group training most frequently was not recovering from its workouts between training sessions, while the other two were continuing to stimulate results while allowing sufficient rest between workouts.

This perspective that less is more is contradictory to what is commonly touted in the world of exercise. But that doesn't make it any less valid.

For most people on regular exercise routines going

nowhere, the most effective remedy for a lack of progress in acquiring strength is to cut the amount of time spent on individual workouts by reducing the number of exercises in a workout, or the number of training sessions per week. When I first started teaching, I recommended that people train three days a week like clockwork: Monday, Wednesday, Friday, then rest on the weekend. Soon enough, I found that most were strongest on Monday, a little weaker on Wednesday, and weaker still on Friday. The following Monday, their strength had returned. I had assumed, incorrectly, that 48 hours between workouts would be sufficient time for the system to recover.

It was clear that those religiously following my schedule were not recovering sufficiently from day to day.

As I learned from experience, my recommended program shifted to twice-a-week training, and those who embraced the reduced regimen showed marked improvement. They needed that extra time to recover, and responded by growing stronger.

Still, the trimmed-down program meets with psychological resistance. Yet, once a woman gets past the idea of more exercise is better, she looks forward to those extra days outside of the gym. She now knows that the rest is allowing her to realize the results that she has stimulated. She is now training sensibly (less), eating sensibly (moderately) and experiencing life instead of reacting compulsively to the roller coaster psyche of eat more- train more.

Most people seeking to build strength train far more often than necessary to achieve their goals. It's bad enough that they're wasting time, but the savage irony is that they are compromising their goals as well. The body rebels at being overtrained.

I believe that if everybody in this country who is overtraining discontinued their present haphazard exercise program and stopped training altogether for several weeks, their overall level of fitness would rise by allowing enough rest to replenish the overall system and decreasing orthopedic problems associated with over-

Ride Or Walk?

Possibly the most physician prescribed exercise is walking. And it has often been stated that walking, and in many instances jogging or running is the best exercise. Really? For what benefits? Yes, walking will in time yield heart-lung benefits (benefits which could have been stimulated safer and quicker with machine circuit training). Jogging and running will also stimulate those same benefits, if orthopedic injuries are not first produced. Those same benefits can be stimulated for the stubborn "aerobics only animal" with proper use (not overuse) of a bicycle (stationary or road variety) with none of the danger – unless you fall off!

training. Doing nothing is no worse, and sometimes better, than following in the footsteps of ignorance. This is not to be interpreted that I am suggesting a sedentary lifestyle – rather I am endorsing a *sensible* lifestyle.

Flip Side

Brief training is two-sided. The other side is intensity. You will not go far in any endeavor if you work halfway. The optimum physical workout is both short and intense.

This does not mean that you race through exercises – quite the opposite. High intensity in this context implies a full measure of control. The routine I will detail is a circuit-type weight-training program commencing with the largest muscles of the body (hip muscles) and proceeding from exercise to exercise to the smallest muscles, without rest. You are not, however, racing against the clock, but performing movements with deliberate speed, working the muscle to the point of momentary "failure," and then moving immediately to the next piece of equipment.

Since this progression quickly elevates the heart rate and keeps it there, improvements in aerobic endurance accompanies the strength-building. Moving from the largest muscles of the body to the smallest at this pace gives all the major muscle groups – plus the heart and lungs – an intense workout. This is the optimal, full-body workout.

> *MYTH: Strength-building exercises do not improve your cardiovascular conditioning.*
>
> *FACT: By applying the proper pace and intensity to a circuit-training workout, you will improve aerobic endurance as well.*

When anaerobic exercise involves doing a set of exercises (say, a shoulder press with a barbell or on a weight machine) and then taking a two-minute rest before the next exercise, the heart rate will fluctuate and the aerobic effect will be lost. But if your circuit-training workout takes you from exercising the body's largest muscles (hips, quadriceps, hamstrings) down to the smallest muscles (in the arms) without pause, you will accelerate the heart rate and keep it there for the length of the workout. There is no pacing yourself through this workout.

Cardiovascular Alternative

Intense exercise for the hips and legs, like the MedX leg press (left), will take the heart rate up to the same levels as running (shown below) without high level impact forces imposed on the musculoskeletal system.

Every exercise is performed to a point of momentary muscular failure. The workout is intense and brief. You are, in effect, strengthening the muscles and bones and improving your cardiovascular system at the same time. This workout style transcends conventional separate aerobic and anaerobic conditioning programs. You potentially realize a third, higher level of conditioning which Arthur Jones terms "metabolic conditioning," – the ability to work your heart/lungs *and* musculoskeletal system intensely and continuously for an extended period of time (20-30 minutes).

Train intensely and infrequently (twice a week), and you can maximize your potential to develop strength, flexibility, and cardiovascular fitness if you adhere to proper form and select the proper resistance level that safely works your muscles to failure on each exercise (Chapters 10 + 11).

Though the very brevity of a training session provides the psychological jolt that revs up intensity, not everyone wants to work quite that hard. Maximum results require maximum effort, and maximum effort reflects a high level of commitment. If you work in a lower gear, you will still make progress but will fall short of your full potential. And no amount of additional exercise time will make up the difference. So time and intensity are inseparable partners on the road to strength.

In no way am I reinventing the wheel here. The strength-building techniques I espouse are not new. These principles, however, have been obscured by the firestorm of useless or outright damaging information that has charred the marketplace – and more than a few bodies – in recent years. My intent is to resuscitate the truth, and explain how it has particular relevance for women.

Potential

It is one of the most elusive words in the English language: potential is the grail that motivated human beings seek. Proper strength training enables you to make significant gains within weeks, and eventually realize your physical potential (optimum levels of strength, flexibility and cardiovascular efficiency) and maintain it by continued training at a high intensity level.

In my program, you will see results quickly, provided that you train with intensity, allow your system sufficient time to recuperate, and watch your caloric intake - the amount of food that you eat. As you approach your full potential, you may find that it becomes more difficult to make gains. But don't make the mistake of increasing your workouts if progress grows stubborn – instead first attempt to increase your intensity of effort.

Even for those who have faster recovery times, the twice-a-week routine is sufficient to reach full potential within the prescribed time. If you don't need the extra work, why do it? There are other things in life to explore.

Time must be your ally – not your master. Train smart and get out of the gym. If your workout reflected an intensity you are proud of, you will never look back.

4. Function Is Everything

The ideal exercise to strengthen the muscles involves full-range movement around the joints.

Low-force intense exercise = safe, effective exercise.

The primary goal of exercise should be to improve "functional ability." Most people, of course, do not think in those terms. For the most part, people exercise to improve their appearance, striving for a hard, taut and lean look. While progressive resistance exercise is the guiding light to aesthetic goals, the real reward is improved functioning. A firmer body enhances your ability to function in everyday life. This program is your ticket to be functionally and aesthetically the best that you can be. Physically, this is what you need to enhance your quality of life.

Anatomy tells us that the muscles support the skeleton and move the body. With stronger muscles and less fat, you'll move better, tire less easily, and sustain fewer injuries. The proper strength-development program also brings improved cardiovascular efficiency, which produces a lower heart rate, which means the heart need not work as hard when muscles propel the body to accomplish a given task.

Improved functional ability enables you to paint a wall with the staying power of Michelangelo, hoist packages and babies without straining your back, keep your edge when a business meeting runs two hours late, and stay focused with a positive perspective on controlling your life. That's what you're after. This is why women should train for strength.

> *Quality of life is a reflection of the condition of your body and mind.*

The best way to improve functional ability is to create stronger muscles throughout their full range of motion (from a complete stretched position to complete contraction), while simultaneously enhancing flexibility and heart-lung efficiency. Your body will thank you.

A muscle gets firmer only when it becomes stronger. When muscles are strengthened, cellulite disappears, limbs assume more shape, and other good things tend to happen. Your body is changing. You can see it. You have stimulated results. No one has done it for you. Meanwhile, life is a little easier for you to negotiate – you function better.

If weight-training is the answer, correctly built weight-training machines provide the safest, surest path to strength and overall fitness and a harder, leaner body. Most efficient of all is equipment that correctly balances and varies the resistance throughout the full range of motion of the muscle being exercised.

This principle – "balanced, variable resistance" – has spawned the quintessential way to train.

A barbell or a dumbbell which, in most instances, does not provide full-range exercise, is still a good tool, but we are looking for the most efficient, safe and sensible way to train for a woman or, for that matter, a man.

Age of the Machine

When it first appeared in 1902, the barbell was a quantum leap forward from the free-hand exercising (wrestling, push-ups, calisthenics, isometrics) that had been the sum of strength training to that point. With its capacity to adjust weights by loading and unloading plates, the barbell stimulated more intense workouts and far greater results. It is still, far and away, the tool of choice in the weightlifting and bodybuilding communities.

Free weights (barbells or dumbbells) are not necessarily the best way to achieve results. The right weightlifting *machine* used correctly will produce all the results of barbell training and more, often times in a safer and faster manner.

The best machines mirror the way the body works. Muscles have specific functions, and when function dictates equipment design, exercise will be efficient.

Nautilus inventor Arthur Jones understood that. Before the advent of his machines in the early 1970's, the barbell was the tool of choice because it allowed people to build muscle in an orderly way, and provided a means to demonstrate strength. Barbell training though, has intrinsic limitations since the barbell doesn't follow the functions of the muscles. Individual movements with a barbell have periods of little resistance and periods of great resistance. Through a complete repetition of, say, a barbell curl, you are moving from a point of virtually no resistance to a point of great resistance, and then back to zero resistance at the end of the movement. Consequently, you are only developing "mid-range" strength instead of "full-range" strength.

> "The movement of body parts caused by muscular contraction is 'rotary' in nature. Barbells provide straight-line resistance. During an exercise, your body parts move through an arc, part of a circle ... resistance provided by barbells is moving in a straight line, which prohibits full-range resistance, and without full-range resistance there can be no full-range exercise."
> – *Arthur Jones, Inventor of Nautilus*

Barbell Curl vs. Machine Curl

Though resistance is provided at the beginning and mid-range position of the "preacher curl," it falls off completely in the fully contracted position, which is the most important position and the only position where there is potential involvement of all the available muscular fibers.

Barbell Curl vs. Machine Curl

Unlike the barbell curl, the MedX machine curl offers a full range of motion for the biceps: Resistance is offered in the stretched, midrange <u>and</u> contracted positions.

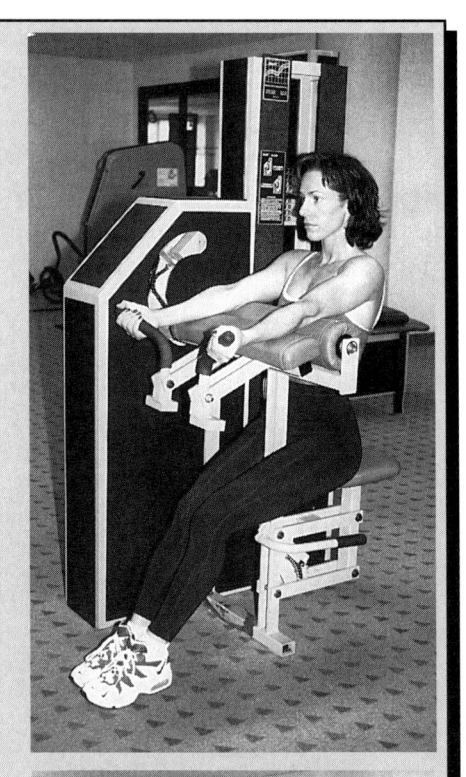

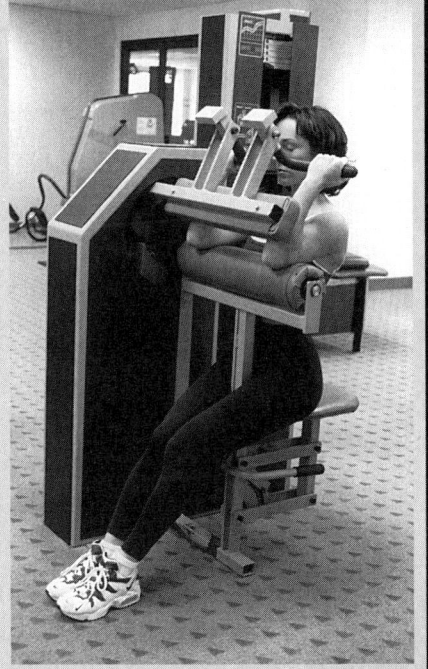

Physics professors and common sense will tell you that a chain is only as strong as its weakest link. Likewise for the muscles. Mid-range training will not sufficiently stimulate a muscle to reach its optimum level of overall strength, safely. It has been suggested that a muscle contracts from its insertion and origin to the center or "belly" of the muscle – from the ends to the middle. If true, then full range of motion exercise permitting resis-

Arthur Jones, inventor of Nautilus and MedX equipment, has been addressing safe, sensible exercise to the public since 1970.

tance at the point of full muscular contraction is the only means of working all available muscle fibers.

The strength of a muscle changes (sometimes dramatically) throughout a full range of movement. A properly designed machine provides resistance while the muscle is in the stretched position, in the contracted position and at every position in between. The muscle must work over its full range of motion – no breathers. It is subject to omnidirectional, balanced resistance in all positions from full stretch to full contraction.

The function of muscles dictates the design of meaningful exercise equipment. Consider the large muscles of the upper back. Their function is to move the humerus, which is the long bone extending from the shoulder to the elbow, downward past the torso. A machine designed to parallel that function provides the optimal way to train those torso muscles because it effectively isolates them, in this case removing the weak link of the arm muscles which come into play in conventional equipment. A similar movement performed with a barbell will inevita-

The chin-up exercise is designed to work the latissimus muscles. However, when the chin-up exercise is performed, the smaller muscles of the biceps fatigue long before the larger, stronger torso muscles are worked hard enough.

bly involve the smaller muscle groups of the arms, which will fail long before the larger torso muscles are worked hard enough.

The chin up is an example of a conventional exercise usually performed in order to strengthen the muscles of the torso (primarily the latissimus, the large muscles of the upper back). Since the chin up directly involves the smaller muscles of the biceps, these muscles will fatigue long before the larger, stronger latissimus are worked hard enough to stimulate the desired result.

Move to other areas of the body. The function of the frontal thigh muscles is to extend the leg. The function of the hip muscles is to move the leg in line with the torso. Correctly designed resistance machines exercise these parts of the body according to their functions. The leg extension, for example, extends the lower leg, and it does so through the muscle's safe range of motion (which movement cannot be duplicated with a barbell). This strengthens the muscle and makes it and the large inefficient knee joint it protects, less susceptible to injury. Again, if we believe that a muscle is only as strong as its weakest link, we have to strengthen the whole muscle – not just part of it. That belief validates what we're trying to accomplish in a sensible, efficient strength-training program: strength throughout a full range of motion.

It is not the purpose of this book to refuel the already burned-out argument revolving around "free weights vs. machines." My opinions are quite obvious throughout the book. If a barbell is your tool of choice, results will be attained utilizing a sensible routine and choice of exercises (see Chapter 11 for sample workouts). However, circuit strength training utilizing machines is a more efficient way to train and applies equally to beginners, the experienced and anyone in between. The only variable is the intensity of effort.

Some machines essentially duplicate barbell movements. These machines will develop an individual's

The leg extension exercise moves the leg muscles through a safe range of motion while protecting the knee joint, making it less susceptible to injury.

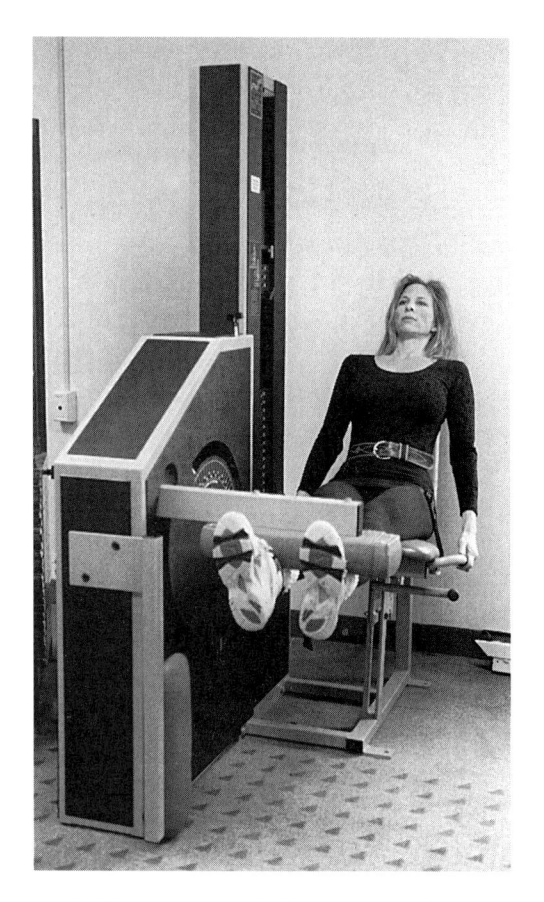

strength, but they are not full-range and do not conform to the functions of the muscles. A bench press machine, for example, is not indicative of how the muscles involved function. Consider that the function of the chest muscles is to move the humerus down and across the torso, and one of the functions of the triceps muscle is to extend the arm at the elbow. When you do a bench press, which aims to develop both of these muscle groups, movement is rotating around the elbow and shoulder joints. Since you are not isolating a specific muscle, it's impossible for you to do full-range work. Because your movements involve more than one axis of rotation, you will ultimately "lock out" when your arms are straight, with the bones taking on the brunt of the load. In this locked-out position, you are not working the muscles very hard, because there is little resistance there – the bones are taking over. Bottom line: potentially more stress on joints, fewer benefits for full range muscular strength.

This does not negate potential benefits from bench presses performed with barbells or machines. Properly executed bench presses eventually will stimulate great strength in the involved musculature. However, this is not the most efficient and safe way to work these structures. The bench pressing movement and other multiple joint exercises can be performed in a very safe and efficient manner utilizing "pre-exhaustation" as I will describe in the "Workout" section of this book (Chapter 11).

In a machine called an "Arm Cross," movement parallels function.

The most popular free weight exercise, the bench press, is usually performed to strengthen the pectoral muscles. However, the exercise provides limited range of movement and the smaller muscles of the triceps will fatigue before the larger chest muscles are thoroughly worked.

The Truth 37

A properly built bench press machine allows a greater range of motion than the barbell bench press and more resistance near the completion of the exercise.

Slow, smoothly performed parallel dips work the pectorals and triceps through an even greater range of movement than the free weight or machine bench press.

You bring the humerus across the torso, and you must continue to work hard even in the contracted position because there is resistance pulling you back. When you lock out in the bench press, as described earlier, you are working around the tool of the barbell (or the barbell-like machine) rather than the function of the muscle. You can try to replicate muscular function and the motion of the body by using a barbell, but because of its limitations, you invariably encounter sticking points. The correct machine, however, provides balanced resistance as strength changes through the muscle's range of motion. The muscles strengthen with no weak links, and the joints receive less wear and tear. That is the beauty of full-range movement around the joints.

Still, the popular notion today is that free weights allow you to build more muscle. However, the truth is – the nervous system does not differentiate overloads

By performing the arm cross immediately before any of the previous chest movements (bench press, parallel dips), the pectorals and related deltoid structures will receive a much higher degree of involvement.

> MYTH: *You can develop greater strength if you train with free weights rather than machines.*
>
> FACT: *Machine circuit training can develop your strength to its maximum potential.*

imposed on the muscles. The nervous system and musculoskeletal system respond when the muscles are exposed to a load that stimulates high intensity contraction, whatever the tool, be it a barbell, machine or a sack of rocks — anything that provides an overload on the involved musculature. A barbell doesn't instruct the muscles to fire their fibers differently than does a machine.

The truth is that a properly built machine will do anything a barbell will and more, with less margin of error, and in a safer, more efficient manner.

Flex Time

The correct workout enhances flexibility as it builds strength. It is important that the two go hand in hand. Unfortunately, flexibility has become a buzzword as misleading as aerobics. The fact is that too much flexibility unaccompanied by muscularity leads to joint instability which, in turn, potentially leads to injury.

Flexibility is important as it allows greater range of movement around a joint. But if you're flexible enough to get into a certain position of stretch, you had better be strong enough to get out of it. If you stretch a muscle, you had better contract it as well. As with strength, the potential for flexibility varies in all women (and men). Flexibility is a result of stretching, and increases in flexibility in our workout are produced when resistance in the starting position of a full range-of-movement exercise is heavy enough to slowly pull the involved body parts into a fully stretched position.

The stretched position of the "dumbbell fly" may put excessive strain on the pectoral and/or bicep muscles.

Whereas there is very little resistance in the position of full muscular contraction, where resistance is needed most.

The arm cross is a far safer and more efficient exercise than the dumbbell fly.

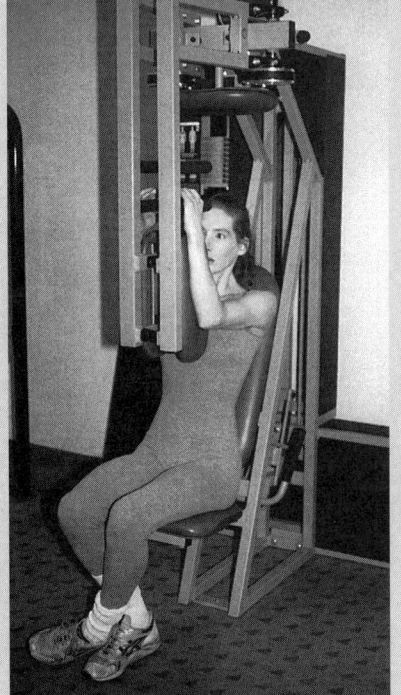

Balanced and variable resistance is provided throughout the range of movement and into the fully contracted position.

In gauging flexibility as well as muscular development, it is valid to compare yourself only against yourself at different times and not against other people. Some people are simply born flexible or with great muscular potential as a function of their leverage systems and muscle insertions. Genetics determines that, and you can't change it.

While there is a biological ceiling on how much muscle mass you can build, most people hover near the ground. You might not be capable of competing with Ms. Universe, but as a woman, you can change the size of your muscles a little and the shape of your body a lot. How this happens is a question of how demanding you are on your muscles and how sensible you are with your eating.

Muscles function according to the principle of "all or nothing": individual muscle fibers at work always push themselves to the max. The problem in terms of muscular strength is that, for most tasks, relatively few fibers are working.

Women in action - the training center of the 21st Century.

> *Exercise, in effect, stimulates the body to respond. Rest allows the response.*

When you lift a light weight, very few of the muscle fibers get the call. If you increase the resistance, you bring more muscle fibers into play. The more muscle fibers involved in the contraction, the greater the potential for strength improvement.

That improvement occurs during the period of rest following the stimulation.

Strong muscular contractions take a toll on the overall system, and if additional similar exercise is performed too soon, before the system has fully recovered, losses in strength will occur.

The same principle applies to males and females, the difference being that a male will stimulate both strength and size increases, while a female will usually experience an increase in strength without an appreciable increase in size. The final product – a harder, leaner you.

The Bones

There is a direct relationship between the functional muscle and the structural bone. The safest way to strengthen the bone is to strengthen the muscle, and sensible training does so in direct proportion while it strengthens the tendons (which connect muscle to bone) as well.

Bone health, understandably, is a major concern for women. A woman who takes a bone density test and then undergoes proper strength training, may show an eventual increase in bone mass. When the muscles lead, the bones follow.

However, the timeworn mentality in some quarters of the medical community has been to recommend "weight-bearing" exercises such as walking and jogging, and ignore true strength training. Weight-bearing exercise does stimulate the bones, but tests them as well. In that testing, if force exceeds structural integrity, injury will occur. Repetitive weight-bearing exercise can often create force that is simply too much for your anatomy to handle. Force overwhelming the body can result from a onetime trauma such as a car accident or cumulative stress.

The greatest sin that an exercise program can commit is to cause injury. Exercise should create a level of force as low as possible to stimulate the desired result. That doesn't mean you should train with paperweights. Properly performed movements on properly designed equipment keeps impact forces low while stimulating your muscles and bones to get stronger. Such exercise, when coupled with high intensity, safely stimulates maximum results.

Do not conclude that, based on the goal of spending the least amount of time to stimulate maximum results, the best method is to do just one excruciating repetition of an exercise. This training procedure is called the 1 R.M. (one repetition maximum) in strength training circles, demonstrating strength instead of sensibly building strength. The 1 R.M. is a necessity for competitive power or Olympic weightlifters who attempt maximum lifts during competition. Otherwise, 1 R.M. is not recommended for a safe, structured strength training program. The optimum program considers the variables of both time and force; if you do one rep brutally hard (high weight, tremendous strain), the involved muscles may not be warmed up, and force production could result in injury.

Instead, for a specific exercise (say, a curl on a machine or with a barbell), start with a lighter weight, do several (8-12) repetitions, and move slowly. Take four seconds to raise the weight, hold the contraction for one second, and take four seconds to lower it – the reduced momentum eliminates jerking or throwing the weight.

Stimulate Results, Not Injury

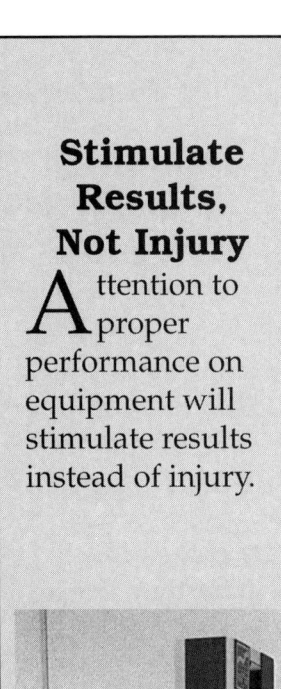

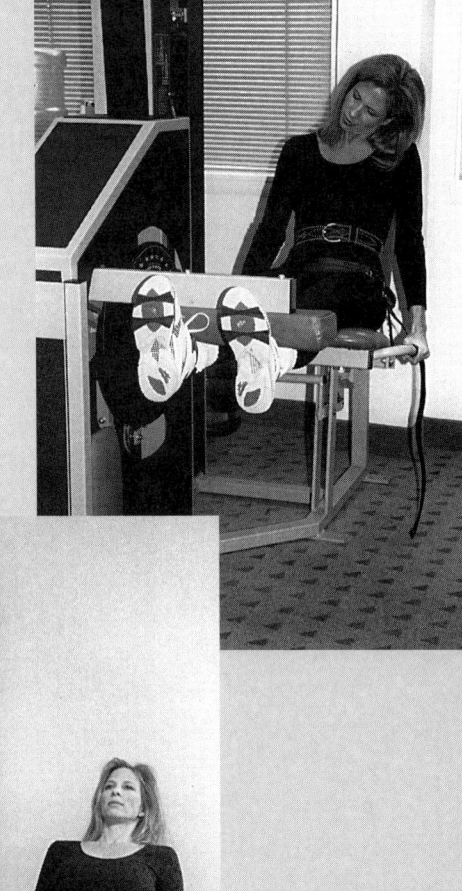

Attention to proper performance on equipment will stimulate results instead of injury.

Example of Leg Extension exercise being performed improperly (above) and properly (left).

This deliberate movement acts as a safeguard against force production exceeding the body's structural integrity to handle it. (See Chapter 11 for full workout sequence).

As you work into an exercise on properly designed machines, subsequent repetitions lower your potential force production and are actually safer for you. Most people tend to avoid the last couple of reps under the mistaken belief that they'll strain a joint or muscle. *But this is the very time when they are less likely to suffer an injury.* The first few reps are actually warm-ups – your muscles are fresh and strong. The last few reps are tough, and with each repetition you are fatiguing rapidly. The safety cushion, however, is greater, because as you go deeper into the set you can no longer exert the force to hurt yourself if proper exercise form is maintained. This is the portion of the exercise that pays the greatest dividends and is the safest part.

The weight should be such that you are unable to complete the last repetition of a given set – this is the condition of momentary muscular failure that safely stimulates the best results.

Expectations

Women ask, as they should, "When will I begin to see results?"

Proper training brings results almost immediately, though they may not be immediately visible. After several workouts and corresponding rest periods, your muscles and connective tissue are already getting stronger, your bones harder.

If you're relatively lean, the visible effects of training will become apparent quickly. Some women carry too much body fat to see their bodies change shape at first – muscular development is hidden by fatty tissue. But that changes with a rational approach to caloric intake and persistent training which raises the metabolic rate.

Muscles are "metabolic" tissue. The denser your

muscles, the faster you burn calories. The woman who has increased her muscle-to-fat ratio (she has become harder and leaner) burns calories much more efficiently than she did when she was heavier and softer. The circuit strength training workout explained in this book raises your metabolism by simultaneously strengthening the muscles, working the heart and burning calories.

How much the body changes is governed, in part, by genetics. One woman may have the potential to make greater muscular gains (in terms of strength and density) than another, but that hardly negates the exercise regimen and the personal goals of the one with less potential. It is folly to compare apples with oranges. Measure

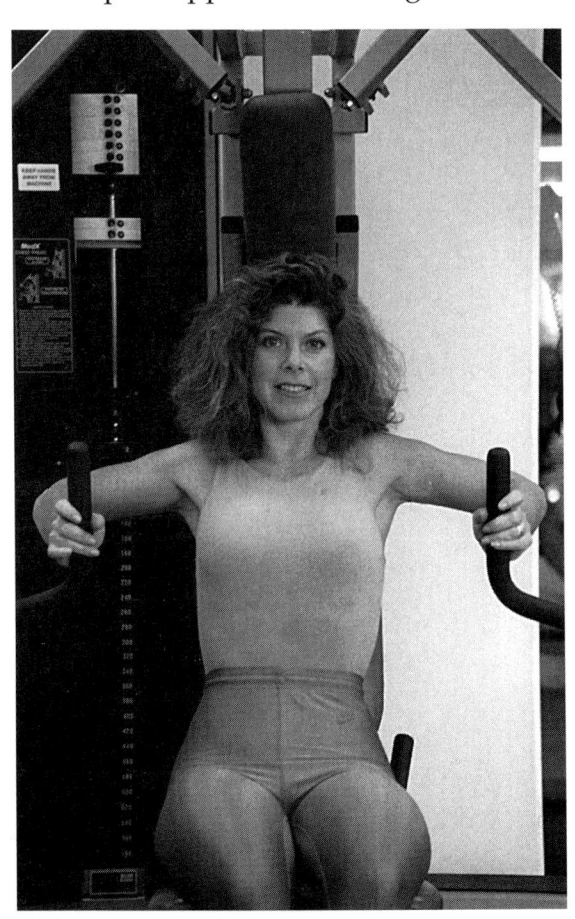

40+ and just hitting her prime.

yourself against yourself, train correctly, and your results will measure up. Everyone can improve!

Trying to determine whether an individual will reach full potential is tricky business. Your age and training history may be just as significant as genetics. Most people start to lose muscle tissue beyond age 40 – that's visibly apparent. A woman beginning a strength-training program at, say, age 50, may not reach a level of strength that she would have attained had she started at age 20. But psychologically, she may not have been ready at the earlier age. Now she is, and she has a different potential to shoot for - to be the best that she can be.

Don't look back; don't second-guess yourself. Women in their 70's, 80's, and 90's realize muscular and skeletal benefits from strength training. The idea is to get started.

If you begin the climb, you'll eventually want to reach the summit. With proper training, you'll reach a certain strength level, and that's about as far as you need to go. Like the championship team that struggles to repeat, you may find it a challenge to maintain that level of strength. If you allow yourself to recede (as evidenced by lighter

80+ years old and getting stronger.

weights, less progression), you're making yourself more vulnerable in everyday living. That is the important consideration in strength training – not the aesthetics. Don't allow yourself to be seduced by the mirror, although you can and should look better - much better. Training is about common sense and practical benefits such as improving functional ability – not narcissism. This perspective fits perfectly with two of our prime goals: the efficient use of time and the avoidance of obsessive behavior.

Once you've reached that summit of strength, depending on your continued motivation, body chemistry and eating habits, your figure may yet gain better definition and you might take on an even shapelier appearance. Again, such results should be anchored to the notion of function. We can equate full potential with the optimal blending of muscular strength and the body's muscle-to-fat ratio.

Some minimal fat, of course, is essential. Fat keeps the body warm, stores energy and cushions friction as the body moves. But, remember, eat sensibly and moderately, you can't flex fat. Muscles move the body.

The expression "She has gone to fat" implies a transformation of muscle into fat. But the body doesn't work that way – muscles cannot turn into fat. But muscles can grow or shrink, and fat cells can multiply.

Many women who exercise in one form or another often feel that they have achieved a "bulky" look which they immediately attribute to building muscles. However, this look is usually a case of just eating too much food. What you are seeing is almost always excess fatty tissue, not muscles. Take a pinch test on an area of your arms, legs or abdominals. Whatever you can pull away from the body is not muscle – it is fat. Try training harder and eating smaller portions of nutritious foods, and watch that bulky look disappear.

If you increase your muscle density (through training)

Senior Citizens

The same training principles apply to every woman, young or old. Only the intensity will vary.

and your muscle-to-fat ratio (through training and sensible eating), you decrease the size of your fat cells and increase the size of your muscle cells. In so doing, you speed up your metabolism (calories burned at rest). You are on your way to reaching your potential. With that higher ratio comes improved speed and muscular strength, a greater degree of quickness, a stronger constitution and a stronger, firmer you. Because there is synergy between the skeletal and heart muscles, as you increase the strength of your musculature, you reduce wear and tear on the heart.

You function better.

5. Bodybuilding: Myths and Missteps

Don't be concerned with developing big muscles – you won't.

Somewhere along the way, a lot of women became convinced that weight training would make their muscles massive and masculine. They wanted to be healthy and strong, but didn't want to compete with their husbands and boyfriends. Some in the fitness field abetted this ridiculous misperception of bulky muscles.

It is extremely difficult for most men, though fueled by testosterone, to develop huge muscles even when they want them. For the overwhelming majority of women – who don't want them in the first place – it's an impossibility.

Most women do not possess the necessary amount of the male hormone testosterone to build muscles of appreciable size. It is false to say that strength training gives women bulky muscles, but in many cases women buy right into this thinking. Too bad, because that approach is the end to meaningful results.

Genetics plays a major role in dictating your potential for muscular development. The key factor is the comparative length of the muscle and its tendon. Most men and women have long tendons and short muscles, which means they can lift and get stronger, but not show great gains in size.

Do this visual inspection: flex your arm as if to show off your biceps. The space between the muscle and the elbow is occupied by the tendon which attaches muscle to bone. The smaller that space is, the longer your muscle belly and the greater your potential to develop that particular muscle's size.

> *MYTH: Strength training produces bulky muscles on women.*
>
> *FACT: More than 99 percent of women do not have the potential to develop large muscles under any circumstances, and those few who do have the potential can develop considerable strength and vitality without metamorphosing into The Hulk.*

Potential may vary from muscle to muscle on the same body. This is why you will see, even among bodybuilders, individuals with massive arm and shoulder muscles, but ordinary looking calves.

The point here, though, is that a very small percentage of the population has the physical endowment to create the physique of a bodybuilder. Those who have long muscles and short tendons are relative genetic freaks. Motivation, intense training and, sometimes, an

Women of the 90's – mentally and physically strong.

extra boost from illegal steroid use enable them to capitalize on their genetic gifts.

True, there are broad-shouldered women who have little surface fat and narrow hips, a combination possibly indicative of a higher male hormone level. (Each sex has some amount of opposite-sex hormone in the blood.) If such women have long muscles, train with intensity, and use artificial aids to raise their already high testosterone levels, they are capable of developing a masculine, muscular look. But that's a lot of ifs, and applicable to only a minute percentage of the female population.

On average, about 30 percent of a woman's body weight is composed of fat; the average figure for males is about 20 percent. Men have the potential to become stronger (and larger) than women because they have a higher muscle-to-fat ratio and higher testosterone levels.

Furthermore, in our society, a man's activity level starting in early childhood promotes muscular development, while women – (sports prodigies excepted) – are not always encouraged to be so active at an early age. Sadly, it is not always a priority in our society for women to get stronger, and this mentality is often reinforced early by the schools. Men, therefore, have the physiological and psychological impetus for physical development, while women sadly languish as second-class citizens with respect to muscles and strength.

But all of this does not negate a woman getting involved full-tilt in a strength-building program, because her only reference point should be herself. Her mind and body are what count – not the perspective of a male-dominated decision making society.

The Body Merchants

Perhaps as an early offshoot of the feminist movement, female bodybuilding competition began in the 1970's, and early events were judged on the basis of muscularity and symmetry.

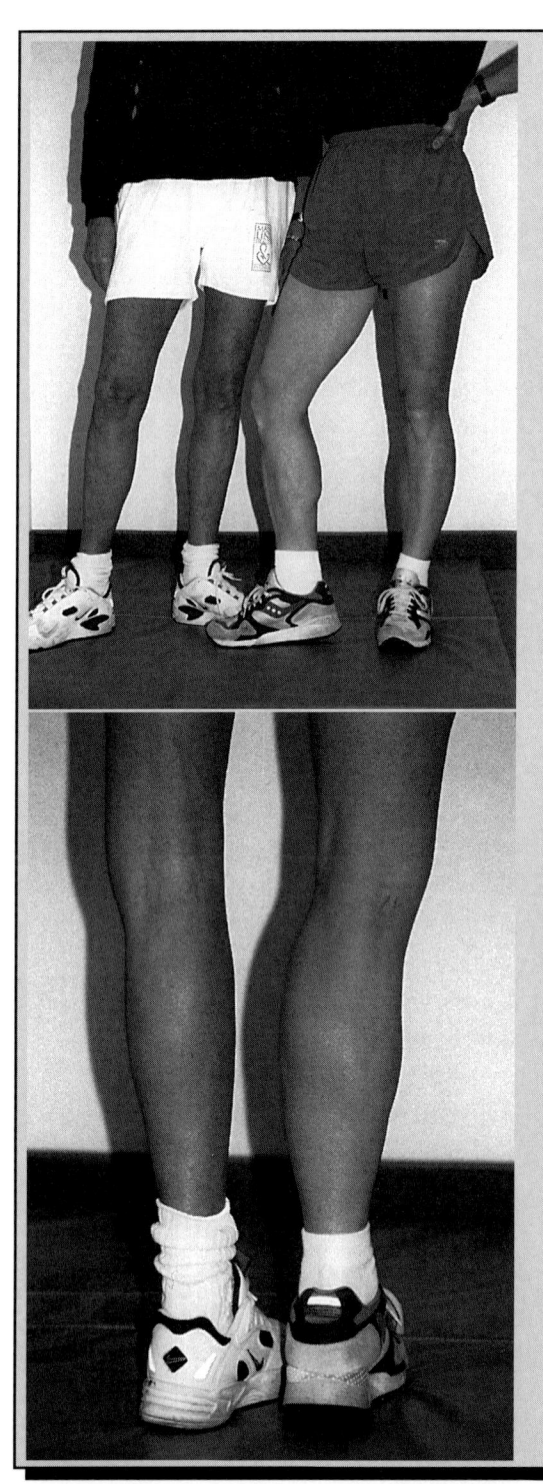

Muscle size is strongly determined by muscle (not bone) length. Regardless of genetic make-up, muscles and bones strengthened by full range of motion exercise will be less susceptible to injuries in sports or everyday life.

Early competition evoked an optimism based on an athletic, lean, hard look which might serve as a healthy role model to society. Unfortunately, as the sport grew, contestants indulged in anabolic steroid drug use to gain a competitive edge. Women already predisposed genetically to a more masculine look further reduced their body fat levels. Breast tissue disappeared, and muscles popped up where they had never been seen before – at least on the female body. In addition to harsher contours, steroids and testosterone substitutes fashioned additional body and facial hair, a deepened voice and enlarged sexual glands. As women bodybuilders built muscle mass, their sport receded in popularity. Early enthusiasm turned to disappointment. Most observers were not wild about the new look. The female body that they found most attractive was tight, lean and hard ... but feminine. Today, the sport appeals only to a small minority, and interest is on the wane.

But that doesn't stop competition winners from dispensing advice, though they are frequently unaware of the true path to health and fitness for most women. Invariably, they talk about how they "graduated" from machines and entered the true bodybuilder's domain of free weights and grueling workouts. In my mind, their graduation was a step backward.

Bodybuilding has always been a subculture. Fans of the sport want to see muscular freaks, and freaks come from those who have the rare genetic potential. In today's competitive reality, that potential is then artificially enhanced.

As a former chief judge of several of the Mr. Olympia contests, I've seen this world up close. Most bodybuilders feel they must get bigger every year, and so they mistakenly spend most of their lives in a gym. Those proffering expert advice have not conducted meaningful research – anyone with big muscles is instantly an expert. And for a price, they'll let you know their secrets:

muscle-building protein powder, energy-boosting capsules, miracle weight-gain, seven-days-a-week split routines, and on and on.

This sort of salesmanship taps the public's gullibility. Merchandisers have sharp eyes for what sells, whether or not it is a valid product.

Some of the gimmickry is laughable. I recall a classic woman's product of the 1970's: a bust developer, a little pink squeezer that did contract the pectoral muscles, but didn't provide enough resistance to change muscularity a bit. For those women not showing gains, it was suggested that they extend the length of their workouts. Instructions specified set after set of exercises performed at different angles, leading to hour-long, worthless workouts. Most women gave up at this point, erroneously blaming themselves for lack of perseverance, rather than the worthless device.

Then there were the popular sauna wraps that sweat off inches and produced smaller thighs. Women soon found, after drinking a glass of water, that their thighs regained their original size.

It has been a case of men selling women on ideas that initially look and sound good, but simply don't work. The quick fix and the fun solution almost always have no validity. Sensible strength training is the road map for you to reach your physical potential and ensure long-term health and fitness.

Women have no need to worry about building big muscles. If you have undertaken a training program and think you're bulking up, get a skin-fold measurement to determine if you're seeing fat or muscle – chances are you still have too much body fat, which continued training and sensible eating habits will reduce. If you do visibly increase your muscular size (the change will be minimal), you'll probably be so happy with your improved overall figure that you'll never look back.

The Female Guru: Circa 1989

While browsing through the crowd at a post-judging local level female physique competition, my wife Elanna and I dropped in on a modern day phenomenon. Near the rear of the auditorium, midway between the stage and the T-shirt concession, one of the afternoon's competitors was holding court for an eclectic group of purists of both sexes, young and old. Some onlookers, obviously novices or late entries into the muscle kingdom had joined in and everyone was tightly gathered around this budding starlet. When someone looks good, people tend to listen. All were anxious to hear the ultimate training methods that one young guru was more than accommodating to divulge.

The potential champ was "ripped," it was clear for all to see. Her 5' 2", 110 pound frame, ultra lean, was proportionate and sinewy. The lights seemed harsh from where we stood and I tried several times to gloss over the coating of acne that lightly covered her skin, undoubtedly the result of anabolic steroids that can also increase facial hair and deepen the voice. Her deeply tanned face indicated no liquid intake for days and looked too nearly like parchment.

Yet, when this lady passed on the "gospel," all were attentive. Though she had trained for less than a year, she took pride in having *sculptured* her entire physique. This, she assured, was without gaining a pound! 110 pounds of rock-like muscle. She mentioned that she graduated from two or three day a week machine training to a much more comprehensive three-day-on, one-day-off free weight double split routine working different body parts daily as do all the champs. She also spoke reverently of a twin sister who, though exercising infrequently, possessed diamond-shaped calves superior even to her own.

Our future champion was witty and eager to respond to all questions. Remarkably for someone with less than a year's experience, she seemingly had the answers to every one. After about 20 minutes under the lights, her acne was glistening, her "tan" was dripping, and despite her undeniable muscularity, she looked somewhat emaciated. Her final response to a query about training injuries centered on the opinion that the top champs train right through the pain, allowing nothing to stand in the way of a title.

With that one, Elanna and I walked away, but not before noticing a striking young woman brush by us. Her face was radiant and her skin fresh and smooth. Her posture was proud and her Lauren dress could not conceal her athletically feminine physique. She literally seemed to walk in splendor. She looked at the one at the center of attention and spoke softly. "Hey, Sis, let's get some dinner before the evening show."

My wife leaned toward me with a slightly mischievous grin and whispered, "She must be the one who never graduated from the machine training."

6. The Right Track

The human system should be trained as it is fed and rested – as a unit.

Most people who train to increase their strength do so incorrectly. I find that I must reprogram men who have trained previously and are accustomed to moving weights around quickly. Such movements do not so much build strength as demonstrate it.

I do not need to explain weight-training misconceptions to most women, since they are usually undergoing meaningful strength training for the first time. I do have to rescue them from the indoctrination that aerobics is the be-all.

Some of the instructional abuses in the field of strength training are almost criminal. For athletes, the notion of "explosive training" – moving heavy weight around quickly in the weight room to approximate the burst of power needed on the field of play – is a perfect example. Visit any training room and you are likely to see people making sudden movements with considerable tonnage. Sometimes the exercise parallels the actual movement required on the field or court, as a basketball player's strapping on weights and jumping in an effort to improve rebounding ability. But no "transfer" will take place here because skill training is specific, while strength training is *general*.

The way to improve in a sport is to practice the skills required by that sport (a runner must run, a basketball player must practice her shot), but simulating those skill movements with weights and other equipment provides no benefit. Few athletes understand that, as they continually seek one more competitive edge. The pros already have their edge: genetics. Strength training is the means to further hone that edge. Proper strength training is safe and works the entire body. Athletes using weights in a gym to simulate their movements on the field tend to use explosive movements that are unsafe.

Take the instance of a rowing coach urging the athlete in the weight room to explode under the weight, in the mistaken conviction that she will row faster as a result of such training. If she follows the advice, she will explode all right – in the knees, lower back, shoulders, neck, etc.

Many strength coaches get their jobs because they have won athletic honors or look good – not because they understand the basic laws of physics.

I should know. In September 1963, I was named an unofficial strength coach at Penn State because I had just participated in the Pennsylvania State Powerlifting Championships. I proceeded to train a football squad of 40 players, and that there were no injuries was a miracle. The only one who made any real progress was a player who was a pre-Med student. His course overload dictated that he train only twice a week instead of the six days-a-week regimen I had enthusiastically mapped out for the players. In 1963, I was still under the assumption that more was better. One day of rest may have been sufficient for the Lord, but not for the Nittany Lions.

Another basic flaw in my football training program was to alternate training the upper and lower body. I figured that the legs would rest while the torso was being worked, and vice versa. But the human system is a unit and should be trained as it is fed and rested. Today, 30 years later, almost everyone in the bodybuilding/strength training field still espouses split workouts, which have become even more specific (the biceps Tuesday, the quadriceps Wednesday, etc.), but are still not the wisest use of your time, nor the most potent way to strengthen the body. By training different body parts on different days, you are demanding that the overall system work when it should be resting in order to realize better results and better shield itself from overuse injury.

Injury Prone

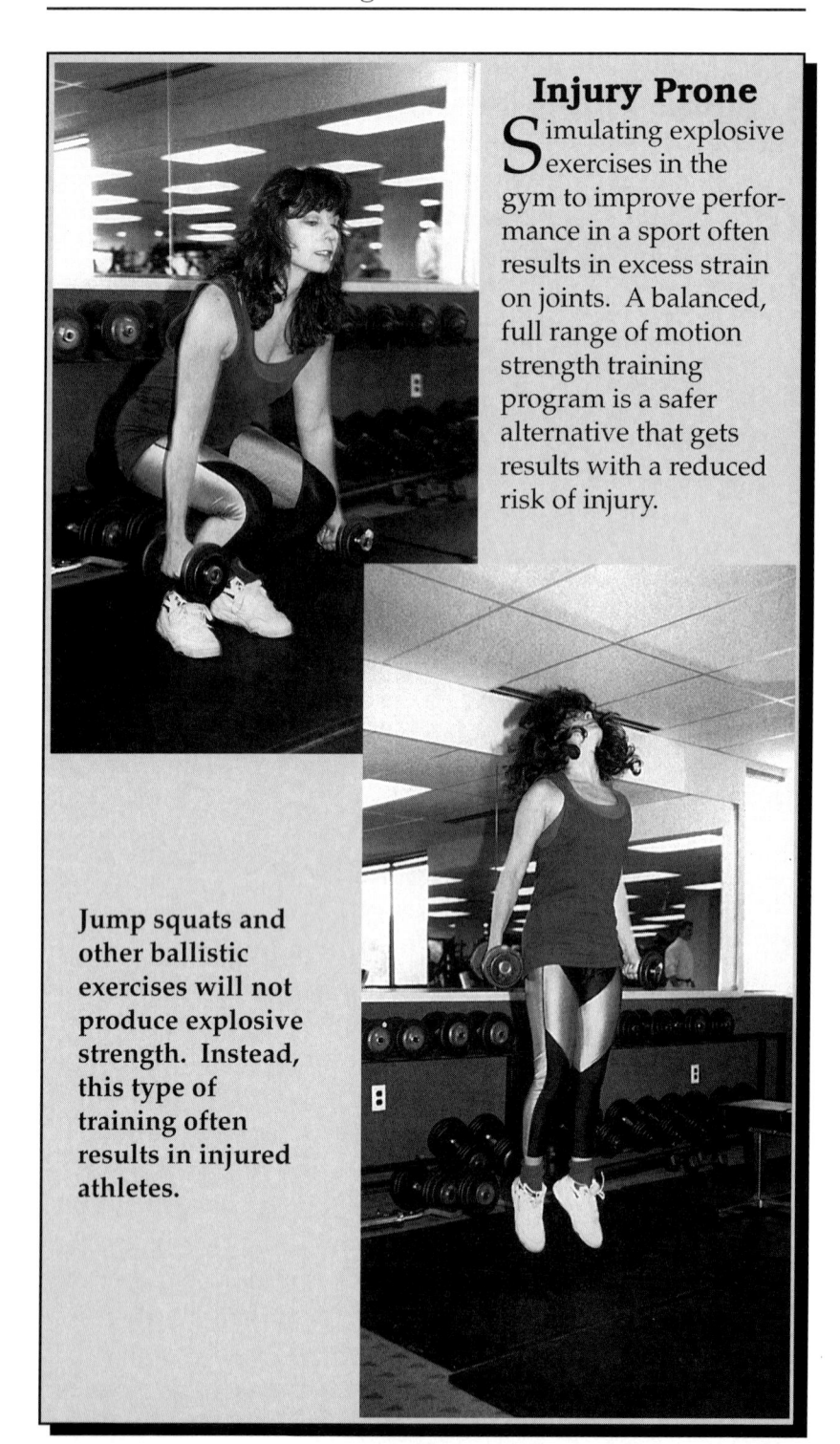

Simulating explosive exercises in the gym to improve performance in a sport often results in excess strain on joints. A balanced, full range of motion strength training program is a safer alternative that gets results with a reduced risk of injury.

Jump squats and other ballistic exercises will not produce explosive strength. Instead, this type of training often results in injured athletes.

Much of the conventional wisdom regarding strength training is not so wise. Much of what is taught from grade school to NFL training rooms is off the mark. I have made that journey and concluded that you should carefully evaluate any suggested training program before embarking on it.

Athletes and Training

Athletes are easily influenced when it comes to performance aids, which often provide nothing more than a placebo effect. Young people then are implored to copy the stars, and that's the way product sales rise. When you train sensibly, include adequate rest periods and eat a semblance of a well-rounded diet, there is usually no need for protein supplements, "carbo fuels" and mega dose vitamins and minerals.

For athletes who use the major muscles of the body, the strength-training workout I recommend is the safest, most efficient route to priming the body for competition. It provides all the physical training that virtually any athlete needs, and its intensity promotes mental toughness as well.

Most sports involve all the major muscles. Working these muscles through their full range of motion is the best way to prepare all athletes for action.

Athletes should train year round, with perhaps several breaks keyed to difficult travel/playing periods in the season's schedule.

> *"Success comes from good judgment.*
> *Good judgment comes from experience.*
> *Experience comes from bad judgment."*
>
> *– Anonymous*

> **MYTH:** *Training different parts of the body on different days will maximize muscular development.*
>
> **FACT:** *Training the body as an integrated unit is the most efficient way to exercise and stimulate the fastest results.*

Split Routines

Split routines are theoretically designed to thoroughly work each muscle. The amount of training in this type of workout quickly leads to overtraining and potentially a loss of strength. A much smarter workout would be the workout explained in Chapter 11 of this book.

Typical Push-Pull Upper Body Split Routine

DAY 1 - PUSH

Chest
Bench Press
Incline Press
Decline Press
"Flys"

Shoulders
Press Behind Neck
Lateral Raise
Rear Deltoid Raises

Triceps
Close Grip Bench Press
Tricep Kickbacks

DAY 2 - PULL

Back
Chin Ups
Rows
Lat Pulldowns

Biceps
Curls
Cable Curls
Reverse Curls

The body will respond as soon as training is resumed, and will quickly return to full strength if too much time has not elapsed. The longer a person has trained, the quicker she'll come back. The muscle has a memory.

Training in season, as well as out of season, serves the athlete best. Why train all during the off-season to build strength, stamina and flexibility, and stop training just at a time when you need it most – during the season itself. In-season training is sometimes a difficult task for the pro athlete fatigued by the rigors of travel and the school athlete juggling a schedule of practice, games and homework. Again, the brevity and infrequency of the workout I recommend make it feasible for the busy athlete.

The regularity of the workout will alleviate soreness. If you are a basketball player, for instance, and you have a game on Wednesday and Sunday, training sessions on Thursday and Monday will bolster your condition – provided that you are engaged in proper training.

For high school coaches to send girls on the athletic field before they've strength trained is negligent in my view. Yet that is customarily the case. Field hockey, lacrosse and basketball players practice their skills, but that's the extent of their physical conditioning. Very few female athletes in this country have any clue about sensible strength training. Once they've been exposed to a good program, their performance level improves rapidly, while sports-related injuries quickly decrease.

In 1980, Olympic swimming coach George Haines (from UCLA) brought his girls' squad east to the Foxcatcher training site in Newtown Square, Pennsylvania. Haines knew the value of strengthening muscle and building stamina before hitting the pool and sought a facility offering Nautilus weight-training equipment and a safe, serious philosophy. During a period of many months, his athletes trained at Main Line Health & Fitness, just outside of Philadelphia. Four years later, the United States Olympic field hockey team followed suit and subsequently won a bronze medal in the 1984 Summer Olympic Games. In both instances, the athletes thrived in a routine that was, at first, alien to them. The satisfaction and results that they derived from their discovery was evident. The energy in the training room was tremendous, yet workouts were structured and safe.

Most female athletes get no such opportunity. When they do have training facilities at their disposal, they

Aches and Pains

If a person works out with any semblance of intensity after a long lay-off (which is not advised), "muscular" soreness will almost certainly be a result. However, if the same exercise is repeated the next day much of the initial soreness will be gone.

While I am not recommending daily workouts, it does seem that the same exercises which make you sore will also reduce soreness. "Muscular" soreness is really a misnomer. Whatever gets sore is probably not the muscles. Connective tissue or fascia perhaps – but not the muscles.

usually find themselves unsupervised in the foreboding weight room. In such a setting, they are destined to lose.

Unfortunately, given the level of ignorance (lack of knowledge) about proper training methods, supervision doesn't guarantee success, either.

Soreness

Do not equate soreness with progress (or lack of progress). Many people do just that, and they are mistaken. When you do an exercise with consistent form, and increase weight and/or the number of repetitions worked to failure, then you know you're making progress. It's a question of getting stronger – not how sore you get.

Nor does soreness from other activities indicate that your exercise program has been ineffective. If you've been training regularly and go skiing for the first time in years, you will likely become sore the day after you hit the slopes. This is probably due to stretching movements to which you're unaccustomed and is a natural phenomenon even for the individual who is in great shape. Similarly, partaking in an aerobics class for the first time may leave you sore the following day. Such a class, while working your heart and lungs, probably has stimulated limited structural benefit, but has subjected you to unaccustomed stretching and joint loading. In neither case does the resulting soreness negate the value of your strength-training program.

7. Psychological Roadblocks

Brief is best.

Because full-range exercise equipment launched more than two decades ago was expensive and the corresponding training highly intense (though brief), full-range training didn't totally convert the public, though many recognized its value. A number of people tried it, then drifted back to more in vogue dumbbell and barbell free weights, easier and longer exercising, or nothing at all. Full-range machines became target practice for the muscle magazines promoting an industry of supplements and conventional equipment.

Meanwhile, the beauty magazines paid little attention to these machines because they figured their readers were not interested in heavy equipment. Physically and psychologically, early machines didn't easily fit women, who were in fact not the design target. Soon after, aerobic impresarios focused on women and cornered the market. Strength training for women was not seen as a marketable concept.

Yet the value of sensible strength training – as embodied in the first line of *Nautilus* equipment – was manifested all those years ago for both men and women. The concept encountered strong resistance then, and still faces an army of naysayers and psychological roadblocks that prevent otherwise open-minded people from traveling the path. Here are the key principles that your brain, as well as your body, must embrace.

Brevity is the Soul of Strength

I have stressed that workouts should be intense, but of short duration and infrequent. This is inconceivable to many people who are programmed to believe that more

Idle time between exercises serves no purpose and has no place in the seriously conditioned woman's workout.

is better. Too much hard training, however, is destructive. And if the body does not break down, it will usually be because intensity has been reduced, thus compromising progress while consuming more time – useless time.

Brief is best. You must earn the brevity, however, by going all out during the training session. A halfhearted effort will yield minimal results.

Failing is Succeeding

The notion of pushing muscles to the point of failure (the inability to complete another repetition in perfect form) – temporary though it may be – is difficult for many to accept. Failure is equated with weakness, and after all, the goal here is strength.

The sensory impact of training on equipment that allows full-range exercise may vary dramatically from free weight exercising. When a barbell movement is completed, resistance has decreased (the lock-out described earlier), and you feel a sense of accomplishment. With the best machines resistance is continuous, and you have to keep working throughout each repetition for the entire set to the point of failure. Full range resistance under load provides a safe and efficient workout for the muscles and bones, but it is difficult for people to accept the prospect of failure at the conclusion of each set of repetitions.

However, if you are results-oriented, get serious about variable-resistance machine training and measure your success after a few months of working to failure.

Eating

It is the bane of most modern Americans, who are blessed with stuffed refrigerators and cursed with the compulsion to raid them. The biggest problem in this country may well be not so much what we eat, but how much we eat.

The best way to get into shape and build strength (and lose weight if need be) is to train hard and eat less of a well-balanced diet. But most people refuse to eat less – or are unable to do so – because eating is the great release, the reward for battling through this harsh life beyond the meal table. Then some of them overload on exercise, believing that they can compensate. They look at exercise as a curative after they have eaten too much.

I see the exercising-for-peace-of-mind syndrome in action quite often at my fitness center. Our busiest day is Monday, when people strap their weekend guilt onto the machines.

The point here is that overeating and too much exercise form a vicious cycle in which the individual is doomed to wasting time and preserving the status quo. True, proper training raises the basal metabolic rate (the amount of calories burned at rest), producing a higher lean muscle-to-fat ratio which, in turn, enables the body to burn calories at a faster rate. But if you keep eating large portions between exercise sessions, you are negating the metabolic gains.

People on such a roller coaster often wonder why they don't see results: namely, a more toned body. Still, the heavier person is receiving benefits from her training – her bones, muscles, and connective tissue are all getting stronger. She'll see outward results when she makes her eating habits sensible as well.

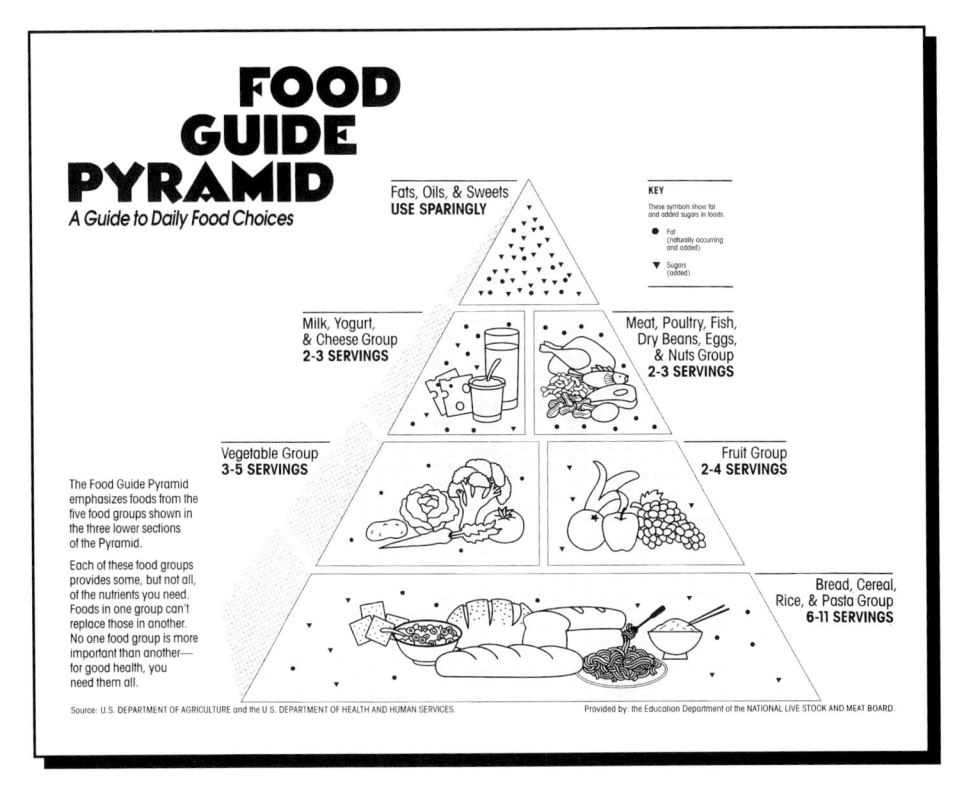

FOOD GUIDE PYRAMID
A Guide to Daily Food Choices

KEY — These symbols show fat and added sugars in foods.
● Fat (naturally occurring and added)
▼ Sugars (added)

- Fats, Oils, & Sweets — **USE SPARINGLY**
- Milk, Yogurt, & Cheese Group — **2-3 SERVINGS**
- Meat, Poultry, Fish, Dry Beans, Eggs, & Nuts Group — **2-3 SERVINGS**
- Vegetable Group — **3-5 SERVINGS**
- Fruit Group — **2-4 SERVINGS**
- Bread, Cereal, Rice, & Pasta Group — **6-11 SERVINGS**

The Food Guide Pyramid emphasizes foods from the five food groups shown in the three lower sections of the Pyramid.

Each of these food groups provides some, but not all, of the nutrients you need. Foods in one group can't replace those in another. No one food group is more important than another—for good health, you need them all.

Source: U.S. DEPARTMENT OF AGRICULTURE and the U.S. DEPARTMENT OF HEALTH AND HUMAN SERVICES.
Provided by: the Education Department of the NATIONAL LIVE STOCK AND MEAT BOARD.

The most efficient way to burn fat is to eat less food! What you eat is important, but how much of what you eat is more important. Eating a wide variety of different types of foods in small quantities will in most cases offer a well-rounded balanced diet recommended by the National Research Council.

Fighting Back

Some women may feel comfortable carrying extra body fat because it relieves them of the pressure to look good and removes the threat of male ogling or worse. In that sense, it is safer for the female not to be in shape in our society. Her out-of-shape body is far less a target of scrutiny and leering. She can disappear into the crowd.

This, of course, is a dead-end mentality. While she edges out of the spotlight, she condemns herself to a life of less vitality – not a very good tradeoff.

Don't let society's tendencies dictate your way of life and, more importantly, your health. Be the best you can be – you owe it to yourself regardless of the reactions of others.

Fun Fetish

Many fashion magazines glamorize workouts as fun and relaxing. If you are seeking fun and relaxation in your strength workout, look elsewhere. Strength training is not about fun and relaxation. Once your body is in better shape, you'll have more fun being alive, but to realize your full potential is serious work.

Again, serious does not mean endless – quite the opposite in enlightened training. The time you save gives you more opportunity to have fun and to live the rest of your life.

If you want recreation, take up a hobby, go to the beach, compete in a sport of your choice. If you're looking for a stronger, harder body to get you there, look here.

Stretching the Truth

Hyper-mobile joints and muscles without balanced strength in their exaggerated range are accidents waiting to happen. There is such a thing as too much flexibility.

Quality of life is a reflection of your mind and body

Good health helps develop vitality improving the quality of life at home, at the office, and with your family. *Quality of life is a reflection of your mind and body.*

Worth the Effort

Some people get an endorphin-high from weight training. Others find weight-training to be drudgery, but force themselves to do it because they realize the benefits. Given the small expenditure of time necessary and the enormous benefits possible, strength training should be done on a regular basis throughout a person's lifetime, incorporated into the routine like brushing the teeth and taking a shower.

High intensity circuit-type strength training is not easy. Body temperature and blood pressure rise, as the heartbeat accelerates, but resting pressure and pulse will decrease in response to the training. It's not a comfortable way for many to exercise, but the results far outweigh the discomfort.

Some thrive on the discomfort and challenge, their self-esteem boosted as long as they compare themselves to themselves and are not obsessed with the body next to them. Comparing one person to another is fruitless because we have varying genetic gifts and limitations.

If you've been training religiously twice a week for three months and compare yourself to a sleek, pantherish model who walks in the gym one day for a little toning, the danger is that you might feel that you don't measure up and your workouts are a waste of time. That kind of thinking would be completely faulty. The truth is that the model has been blessed genetically, and can do everything wrong and still look good, or can do everything right and look even more fantastic. Compare yourself only to yourself, and you'll find significant improvement. If the change is not strikingly visual, which it can be, know that your underlying skeletal and muscular systems have been strengthened; you can prove that on the machines. Your intensity and comparing you to yourself is the barometer – not someone else's body, not a magazine cover.

Disregard the exploitation pushed by women's magazines – the simplified suggestions for women who really don't want to do much of anything serious in terms of exercise. Embrace the serious program – high intensity, yet safe and not time-consuming. The challenge is worth it. And so are you.

8. Battling Nature

Strength training can help a woman neutralize the joint instability brought on by potential childbirth.

When a woman reaches her child-bearing years, her body changes whether she delivers or not. Significantly, ligaments in the hip and pelvic girdle start to stretch. To make way for baby, the area becomes more flexible – nature is accommodating in that way. The woman's bodily structure is altered to allow her to carry, and then deliver, a baby.

The real problems can come afterward. For as it re-shapes a woman's body to give birth, nature leaves that body in a weakened condition. The laxity in the joints remains, and most women never do anything to strengthen the hip area stretched beyond its original boundaries.

Fast-forward to menopause, loss of estrogen, and the accelerated loss of bone mass in the post-menopausal years. The hip, femur, and spine become highly susceptible to fracture. The woman suffers a trauma, the fracture occurs, and the outcome may be replacement surgery or lengthy medical treatment that never needed to happen had she followed – all those years – a strength-training program to strengthen the hip girdle.

Prevention First

Strengthening the major muscular structures (and the connective tissue and bones) including the entire hip girdle through full-range of motion medically oriented exercise is <u>the</u> major factor in preventing fractures in post-menopausal women.

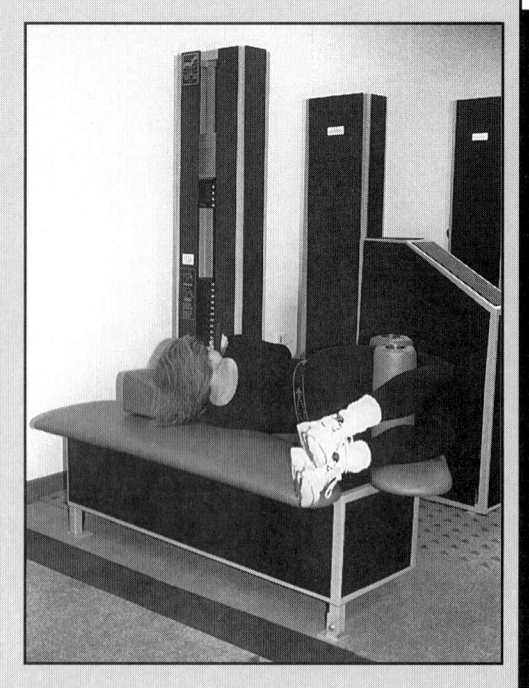

Full-range exercises for the hip – Hip Extension (above) and Hip Abduction (below)

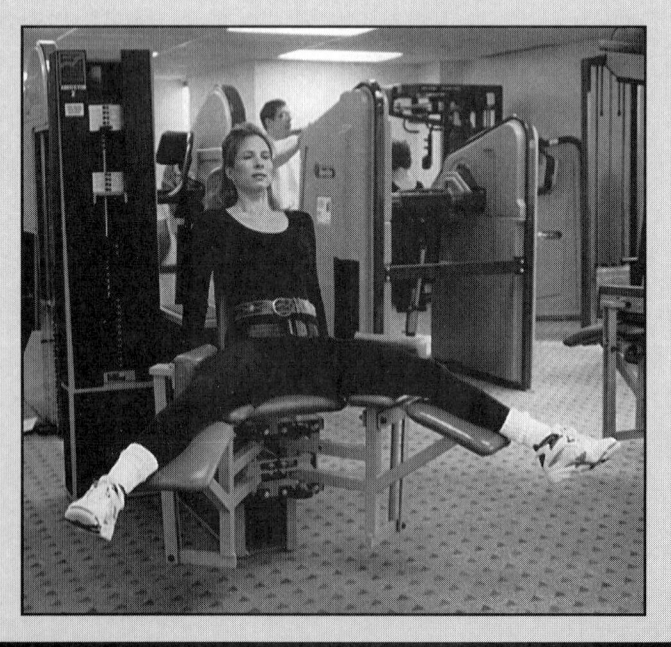

Once created, the joint instability in many women lasts a lifetime unless neutralized by serious, sensible weight-training. Hip replacement is in many hospitals the most performed surgery on a yearly basis. Before books such as this were available, there was little meaningful advice published for women differentiating aerobic activity and sport (be it recreational or competitive) from serious strength training. It is this serious business of meaningful exercise that strengthens those muscles around the vulnerable hip joints and every other joint. The constant pounding of various aerobic and sports activities places potentially dangerous high impact forces on the joints.

This concept of women training to parry nature's assault on the female anatomy is totally overlooked in our society; training should start as early as puberty. It is effective because proper training *strengthens the bones* as well as the muscles.

Strength training is also appropriate for a healthy woman during pregnancy, and common sense would suggest that the strength acquired can aid in delivery.

Staying strong during pregnancy lowers orthopedic risks associated with hormonal and postural changes.

> *It has been my observation that high impact aerobic exercise can lead to uterine prolapse in the non-pregnant state and in the first trimester of pregnancy. A safer, smarter fitness alternative would be a structured, full range of movement strength training program performed in a medically oriented fitness facility.*
>
> *– S.H. Bailey, M.D.*
> *Obstetrician/Gynecologist*

Most conventional pregnancy programs center on low impact type aerobics. In reality, however, most women have had little trouble delivering a baby because they could not breathe, but some have had tremendous difficulty because of orthopedic problems that could have been avoided by the proper training program. Delivering that baby will, in many instances, be quite a bit easier if there is greater strength in the entire gluteal/hip area.

The correct strength-training program works for pregnant women, the young, the old and everybody in between. Of course, intensity levels and benefits derived will vary, but benefits can be realized across the spectrum of women.

Until recently, the medical community has shown little apparent interest in the value of strength training for women – for years, exercise guidelines set by the American College of Obstetrics and Gynecology focused on aerobics. Muscular strength was not a priority.

What should be the priority for women is the most efficient full-body workout possible, one that strengthens the bones and muscles along with the heart and lungs, yet does not tax the joints. Because of ignorance and the tendency to cling to myths, women – pre, postpartum or pregnant – in obvious need of strength-building are often told simply to "walk." That's it for the exercise prescription.

Nine months pregnant and still training.

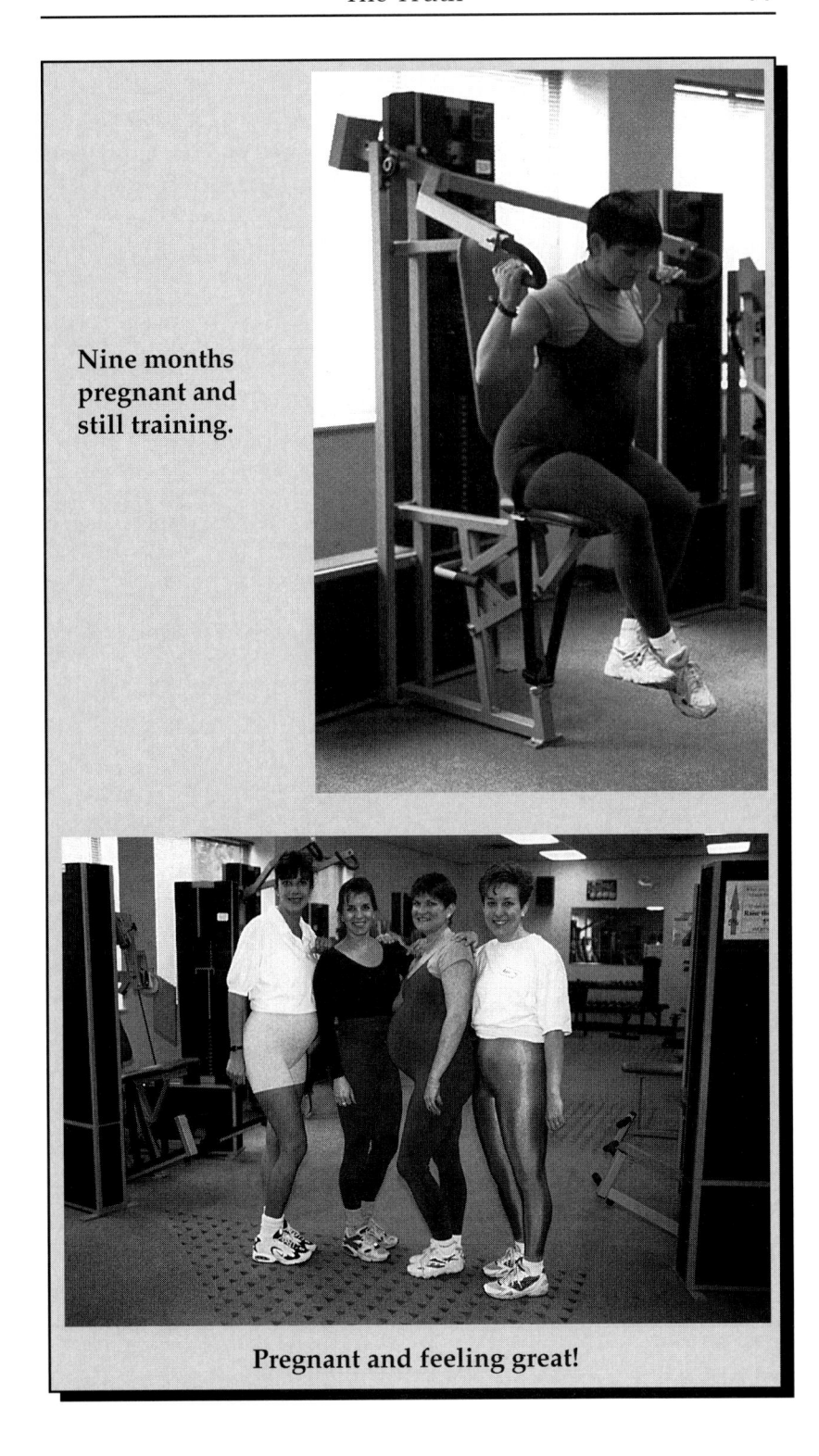

Pregnant and feeling great!

A walk in the park on a spring morning is a nice pastime, but it's not enough to strengthen the body for the marathon of pregnancy/delivery or the recovery from childbirth. Given the postural changes wrought by pregnancy – the shoulders slumped, the lower back torqued – and the increased demands upon circulation, the benefits of training become even more timely. Of course, during pregnancy, exercise intensity is reduced as merely maintaining strength is the primary goal at this

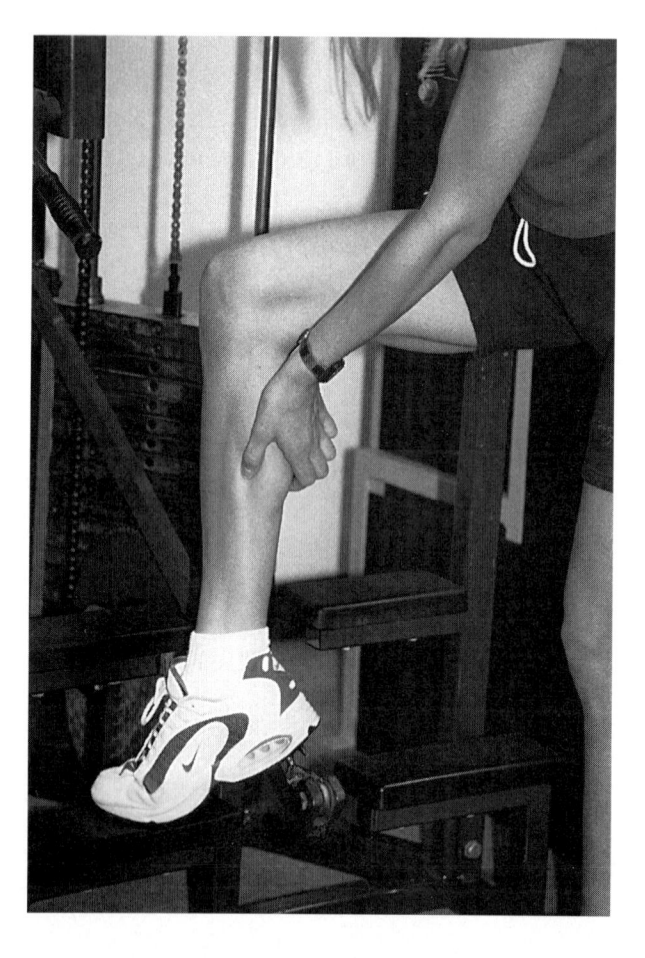

Structured hip and leg exercise throughout pregnancy improves circulation below the baby, alleviating cramping and varicose veins.

time.

The orthopedic benefits of strength training should make it the central part of the exercise regimen during pregnancy, though much of the medical community relegates it to second fiddle behind aerobics. Correct strength training involves no jarring forces which are potentially damaging. Much aerobic exercise cannot make the same claim and does little to strengthen muscles, connective tissue and joints.

Turning Back Osteoporosis

In a 1991 consensus development conference on osteoporosis, the condition was defined as "a disease characterized by low bone mass and microarchitectural deterioration of bone tissue, leading to enhanced bone fragility and a consequent increase in fracture risk." Simply stated, osteoporosis is bones that become porous, structurally weak and are susceptible to fracture. Osteoporosis affects more than 24 million people in the United States, primarily women, thus making it one of the most prevalent diseases. Osteoporosis causes 1.5 million fractures annually in the United States.

Studies have shown that stress fractures of the pelvis are a particular problem for women joggers over the age of 30, which I believe underscores the need for women's strength training and the mistake of overdoing aerobics.

A sensible, high-intensity, strength-training program increases bone density as it builds muscular strength. An increase in bone mass means an increase in bone strength, and stronger bones are less prone to degenerative disease.

That should be a major consideration even for young women who need to recognize the problem they eventually must confront. Of course, it is not an easy message to communicate to a 20-year-old whose immediate thoughts are not about menopause, loss of estrogen, calcium depletion and crumbling bones.

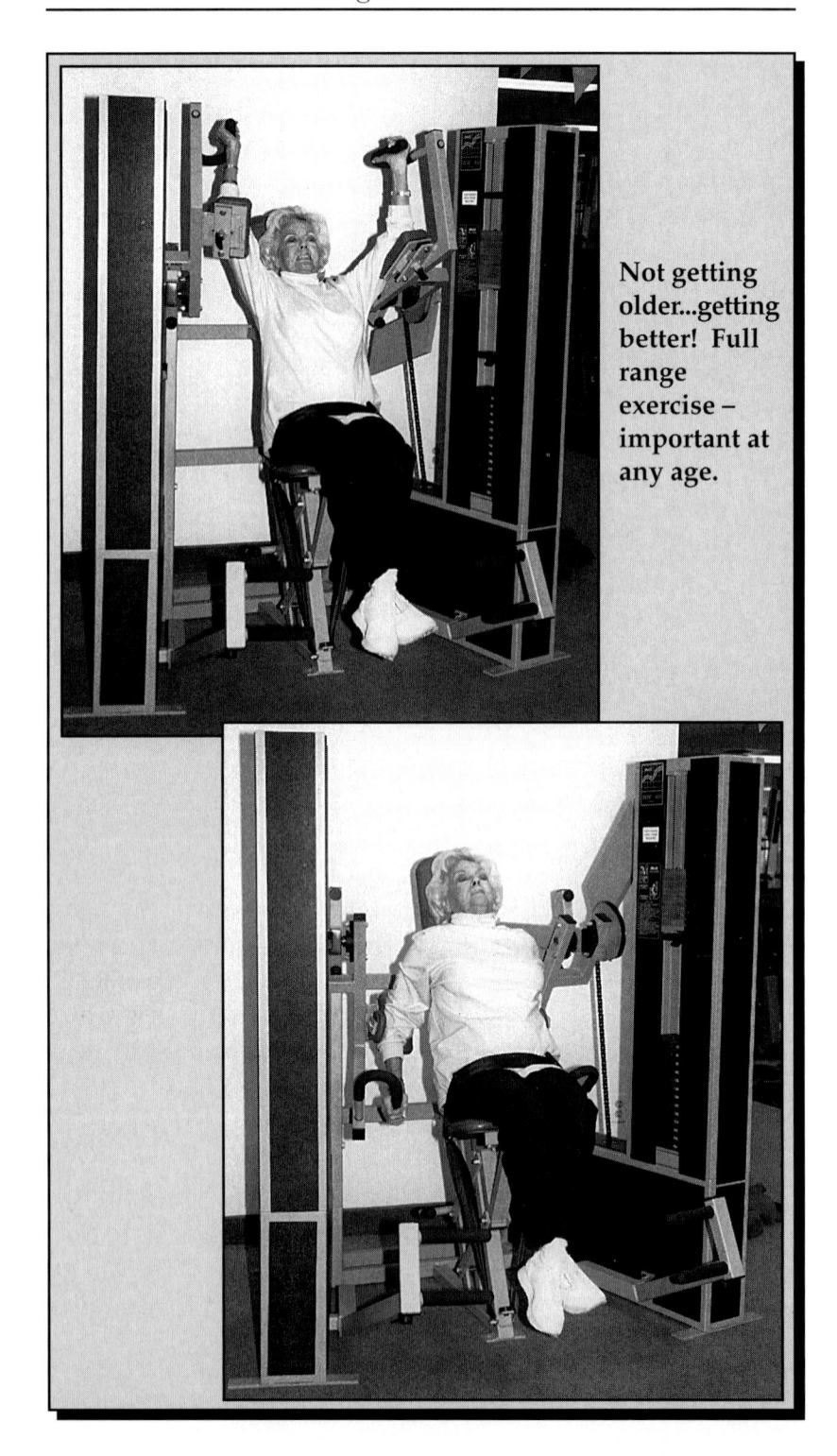

Not getting older...getting better! Full range exercise – important at any age.

> **"I Don't Want To Build!"**
>
> How many times through the years have I heard a woman say, "I don't want to build, I just want to tone"? As if building large muscles happens quickly and automatically once a woman touches a weight. The truth is that <u>every</u> woman should strive to get as <u>strong</u> as possible! Forget aesthetics for a moment, there are no huge muscles in your future, only strong muscles. Remember, stronger muscles mean stronger and harder bones. And if you have defined the word "osteoporosis," you will want to build, build, build! Osteoporosis is a crippling yet silent disease – a potential killer. Forget big muscles, remember hard bones!

The medical community has placed the dialogue primarily in a laboratory context: raising estrogen and calcium levels via medication and supplements. Most women then conclude that, if they can take a pill, why lift weights?

Hormone replacement therapy and new pharmaceutical drugs, although important, will not increase vitality and are not effective in strengthening the musculoskeletal system. Strength training is the most efficient way to combat bone demineralization and retard osteoporosis – empirical evidence and common sense show this to be the case.

Why is this so?

Consider what happens to strength and body composition with the aging process. As sedentary individuals become older they will lose 10 to 12 percent of their muscle mass, 20 percent of their muscular strength, and 20 percent and 30 percent of their cortical bone thickness for males and females, respectively. The loss of muscle mass will account in part for a decline in the basal

This is the way grandmothers are looking today.

metabolic rate and body fat will increase. The loss of muscle and increase of body fat can occur with no appreciable change in absolute body weight. This scenario can be a sneaky process with the scale reflecting a number that makes us feel deceptively comfortable. Still, regular exercise is outright avoided by many. To the 22 percent of the American population that exercises regularly, exercise and its potential benefits are being taken more seriously. The search for the Holy Grail may actually be attainable, but it will come with a price. For when the truth is revealed, when we learn to differentiate exercise from recreation, we will only then recognize that meaningful exercise – exercise that stimulates results in functional ability; improved strength, flexibility, and cardio-respiratory conditioning – is actually a means to the end.

This work is necessary to take us to those quality later years in life which can be enjoyed with dignity and free of aches, pains, stiffness and lack of mobility.

While most people think of bone as rigid and inert, it is dynamic organic tissue that responds to forces imposed upon it. Muscles, which are connected to bones via tendons, relay forces to the bones. As the muscles respond to force – including that created by exercise – so do

Strengthening the upper back musculature by retracting the scapula, as shown in the exercise above, will help ensure good posture and reduce potential problems later in life relating to fractures of the vertebrae.

the bones. Sensibly strengthening the muscles strengthens the bones as well – without testing them to potential destruction.

An increase in bone mass is generally thought of as an increase in cortical thickness; that is, an increase in the thickness of the outer shell due to the formation of new cells. But fortifying the bone also means maintaining its "microarchitecture," the spongy bone marrow and network of supportive structures beneath the outer bone.

To visualize this, think of pillars from a typical structure in ancient Rome. If you place a load on a single column and then increase that load, the column may collapse. Add a cross beam anchored on another column, however, and the greater weight will be supported. Bone tissue functions – and is constructed – in similar fashion.

Bone remodeling occurs throughout life. When the bones are breaking down faster than you can rebuild them, you're in trouble. A loss in cortical thickness in women begins around age 35, and they will lose about 30 percent of that outer shell through an average lifetime if

The "secret" is revealed. Progressive weight training is the <u>best</u> way to strengthen muscles and <u>bones</u>.

undeterred by training and/or medication. During the same span, the inner bone also starts to degrade, to get porous. Conditions such as the "dowager's hump" may result from the accumulation of small fractures of the vertebrae. Worse, deteriorating bones may trigger a fall and serious injury.

Strength training can keep the structural cross beams in place. As the muscles are strengthened, so are the bones. When a young woman takes up strength conditioning, she is taking out an insurance policy for her later years; she is effectively pushing back the onset of osteoporosis. Though a woman past menopause may be hesitant to start training, she is certainly not too old to realize benefits.

Many in the medical community, however, still see weight training as faddish or narcissistic rather than of functional value to the body. I don't think that perspective will change quickly, despite a study published in the December 1994 Journal of the American Medical Association saying that twice-a-week, 45-minute weightlifting sessions provide more benefits to the bones than estrogen-replacement therapy in terms of decreasing the risk of osteoporotic fractures due to a fall.

I've been saying that for 20 years.

Arthritis

For most people, age brings joint wear and tear which means less shock absorption and reduced mobility; calcium buildup may deform the joint, producing gnarled knuckles and stiff shoulders.

Patient: _____
Date: _____

DIAGNOSIS:
Arthritis

PRESCRIPTION:
Rehabilitative Strength Building Exercise.

We call this condition arthritis, and its impact ranges from irritating to debilitating.

External forces can worsen the arthritic condition, especially in the spine. High-impact aerobics can make matters worse. Arthritis is the product of years of joint-stress accumulation (a silent process, remember), and the arthritic patient is particularly susceptible to further stress. Strength training, however, can reduce or even alleviate symptoms of arthritis in many cases because it increases muscular strength and range of motion around the joint. If done properly, it produces none of the jarring force of most aerobic exercises. If arthritic type degeneration is a factor in your life, get involved under supervision of someone who understands the concepts presented in this book.

Cellulite

Dimples on the cheeks may prove irresistible, but they're less than welcome on the thighs. So goes the tale of woe known as *cellulite*.

When subcutaneous fat tissue bulges the skin, the cottage-cheese look emerges. For women, the most susceptible areas are the buttocks and thighs. The good news is that a strength training regimen can reverse this condition.

An experiment conducted in the fall of 1994 by WCAU-TV (CBS) Philadelphia tested the effectiveness of three different approaches to reducing cellulite. While this was not a rigorous scientific study, the anecdotal findings of Pennsylvania Hospital dermatologist Susan Taylor, M.D., were significant.

The battle was for nothing less than the soul of cellulite. Dr. Taylor examined photos of three women, each of whom then tried a different method to rid herself of cellulite. One woman underwent a liposuction procedure, a second rubbed "reducing cream" on her thighs, and the last engaged in a program of strength training of two sessions weekly. Three weeks later, the women returned in the flesh for a look-see by Dr. Taylor.

The results were dramatic. According to the physician, the woman who had received liposuction showed a decrease in overall fat (after all, fat had been vacuumed out of her legs) but no reduction in cellulite. The woman who had used cream was virtually unchanged. The exerciser, however, showed a marked decrease in cellulite – her thighs were indeed tighter, firmer.

A second visual inspection came three weeks later. According to Dr. Taylor, the exerciser showed additional improvement, the woman using thigh cream had a slight decrease in cellulite, and the woman treated by liposuction had no apparent decrease.

Interestingly, the latter two contestants did begin their own strength-training programs after seeing the gains of the exerciser at Dr. Taylor's first in-person evaluation and any results obtained can probably be attributed to the exercise program.

The winner of the contest had completed a series of basic weight-training exercises that I prescribed and supervised. Her workouts were solely on machines described in the last part of this book, and separate aerobic exercises were not part of the program. Her winning appearance was the result not of losing fat, but of flattening the dimpled look with stronger muscles and tauter skin.

Cellulite was conquered. The subject's visual improvement is even more impressive when you learn that she has suffered throughout her life with hypothyroid – an inactive thyroid which hampers weight loss – and an arthritic condition which yields daily pain.

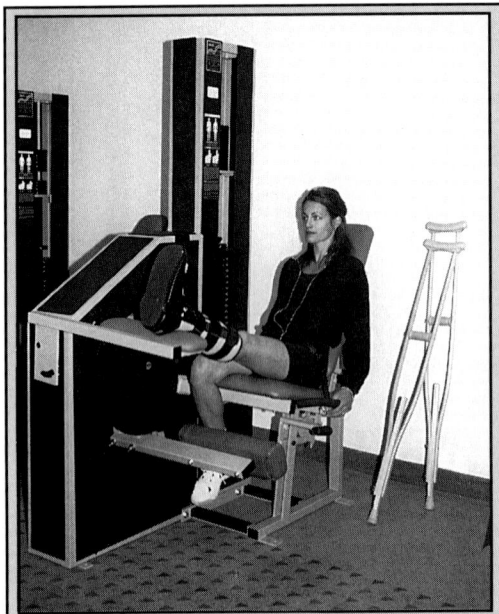

Rehabilitation

The body functions as a unit. Training the uninjured limb and the rest of the body will speed rehabilitation of an injured limb through a process known as "indirect effect."

9. Rehabilitation

It is usually easier to rebuild the injured soft tissue of a trained individual than it was to originally build that same muscle.

Not long ago, after suffering for years from a football-related torn rotator cuff, I underwent major surgery. Subsequently, my right arm and shoulder atrophied immediately and immensely after being immobilized for a period of time. I resumed training when my range of motion permitted, and my strength and size quickly returned to their previous levels. As noted earlier, the muscle has a memory.

Not that rehabilitating a muscular injury is a Sunday picnic. Whether you are involved in regular training or rehab, you must put forth the effort to realize results. But today's sophisticated equipment has removed much of the uncertainty surrounding rehab programs and reduced the reliance on surgical procedures.

Possibly, the two busiest rehabilitation sectors of the human body are the neck and lower back, and most problems can be alleviated by exercise rather than surgery. There are now available rehabilitative exercise machines built to safely strengthen these areas with an efficiency not possible before.

Aching Backs

Everyone, it seems, develops a sore back at some time. In most instances, the condition can resolve itself. But in some cases, it can become chronic or even disabling. By some estimates, the total cost of lower-back problems in this country is in the tens of billions of dollars.

Whatever the culprit, the muscles are often the answer. In most people, these muscles are comparatively weak, and the eventual result is pain or worse, leaving the spine vulnerable to acute injury or a chronic buildup of pain throughout everyday life. Everyday movement of the lower back involves the muscles of the hips, thighs, obliques and abdominal area as well as the back itself.

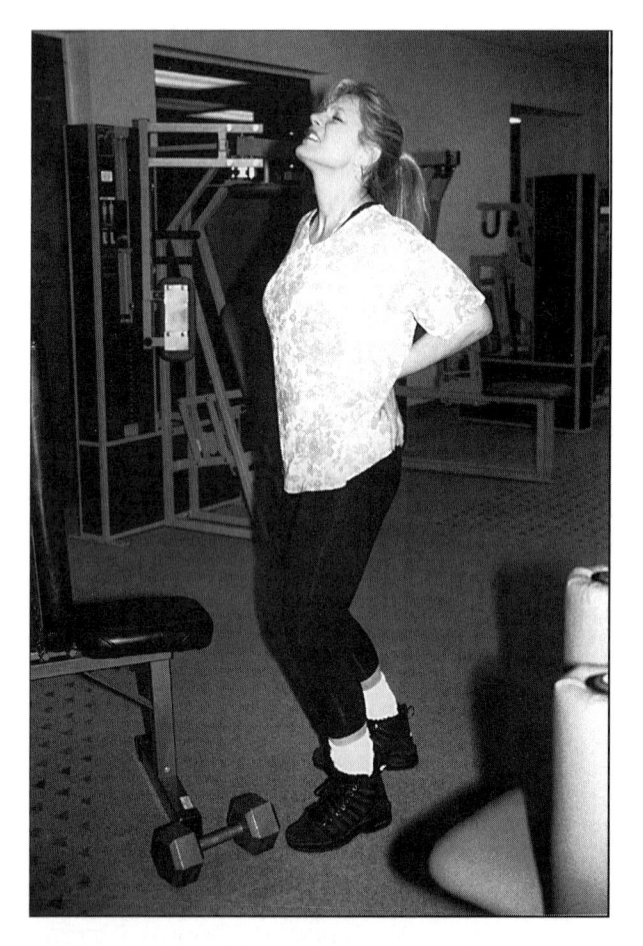

Over $40 billion annually is spent on treating lower back injuries. Much of this cost could have been avoided if proper attention was focused on strengthening the muscles that extend the lumbar spine.

Lower Back Strength Training

Direct exercise for perhaps the most vulnerable area of the body, the muscles that support the lumbar spine. A must for women of all ages concerned with preventing and combating osteoporosis.

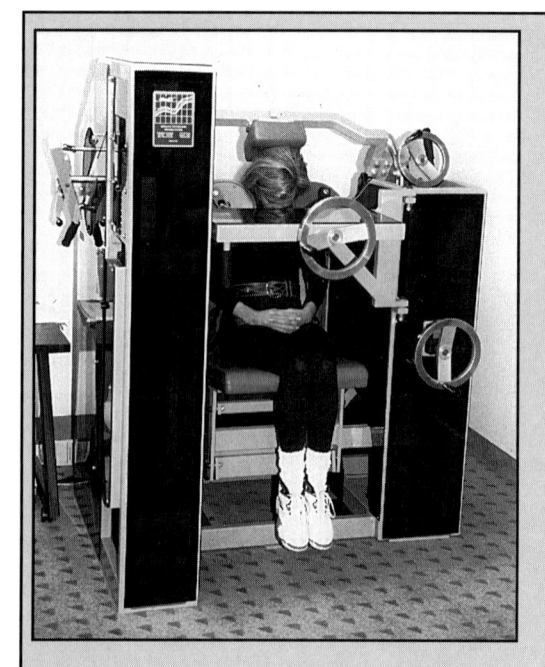

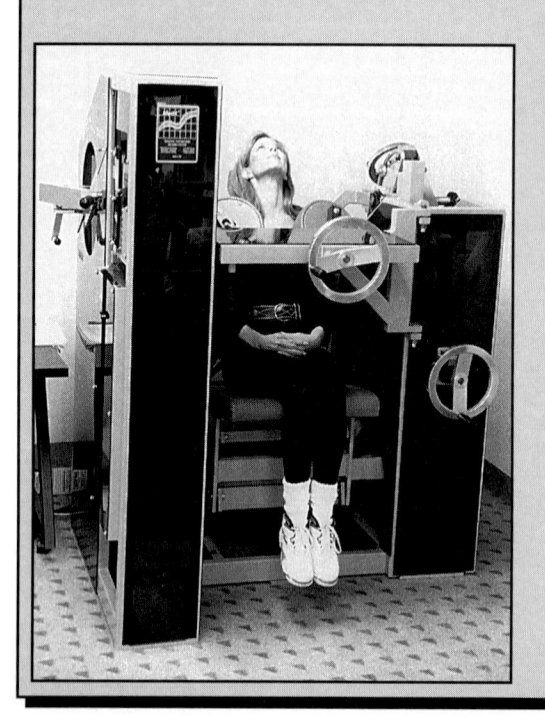

Cervical Spine (Neck) Exercise

The soft tissue of the neck is often incapable of supporting the stress placed upon it. State-of-the-art rehab machines are designed to strengthen the neck muscles which help alleviate physical and psychological stress. The antidote to rehabilitation is to keep the neck muscles strong in the first place.

Those lumbar-extensor muscles are the weak link (again, the chain is only that strong), and when forces imposed become too great ... you know the result.

Almost the same situation exists in the cervical spine (neck), where the soft tissue often is incapable of supporting the stress placed upon it. I am speaking here of the physical stress found in a daily agenda of lifting objects and other various everyday chores. The accumulation of these mundane forces – let alone something as traumatic as an industrial or automobile accident – is enough to throw many of us out of whack. In addition, psychological stress in women with less physical strength often manifests itself in neck and trapezius spasms.

State-of-the-art rehab machines are designed to isolate the muscles of the lumbar and cervical spines, whereas earlier equipment involved the larger muscles of the hips, thighs and torso. Isolation provides the most efficient route to rehabilitation. One or two brief exercise sessions weekly – or even biweekly – can bring optimal results (sounds miraculous, but it's true). Take the case of the woman who is entering her 40's or 50's and finds that some everyday tasks – functions previously taken for granted – are now causing physical stress. Her back aches, neck pain that used to be sporadic is picking up in frequency and intensity. This is the possible result of degenerative change and the weakening of the soft tissues of the body. In most cases, the condition is the result of not maintaining the strength of the muscles that move the body and support the skeleton. The antidote to rehabilitation is to keep those muscles strong in the first place.

Once the need for rehab is established, the options are usually exercise or surgery. In virtually every case, surgery for chronic lower back or neck pain should not be performed until a progressive exercise program has been undertaken and proven ineffective. Surgery, then, is the last resort and will be necessary in some instances. In many cases, however, the exercise program will not fail, and the woman will be able to strengthen her muscles around the joints sufficiently to resume her everyday functions.

Beyond Therapy

Many women who sustain an injury are unaware of meaningful training programs – that may have been the reason they became injured in the first place.

Once the rehabilitation sessions have ended, it is important that patients learn how to incorporate a safe, structured fitness plan into their lives. I would strongly suggest for every woman initially seeking either sensible fitness or safe rehabilitative exercise to carefully choose a *medically oriented fitness facility* which will give priority to the cause and effect of meaningful exercise as stressed throughout this book.

Once involved in proper exercise, they may not need rehab again.

THE WORKOUT: Principles

1. Sensible Training = Maximum Results
2. Slow Go
3. Fast Pace
4. Get Stronger
5. Use The Machines
6. Keep It Brief
7. Train To Failure
8. Pre-Exhaustion
9. Workout Frequency: Never More Than Twice A Week
10. Record Keeping
11. Stay Focused
12. Even The "Ideal" May Be Too Much
13. Diminishing Returns
14. Rest and Reap The Rewards

III. The Workout

10. Principles - Realize Your Potential

Sensible Training = Maximum Results

Some of the following principles that underlie strength training are summaries of topics already covered and I believe worth repeating. The last several principles pertain directly to the workout itself, which follows in the next chapter.

Slow Go

You can never move a weight too slowly, but you can easily move it too fast. If you are ever in doubt about your speed of movement, slow down. Fast movement may subject muscles, connective tissue and bones to high levels of impact force.

On variable resistance machines, you should take about four seconds to complete the positive (concentric) phase of the exercise, pause in the contracted position (in single joint movements) for at least a second, then take another four seconds to complete the negative (eccentric) movement. "Positive" refers to the lifting part of the movement, "negative" to the lowering part of the movement. Lowering the weight may be the most important part of the exercise and should be performed with the same concentration as the lifting phase of the repetition.

Fast Pace

Although repetitions are performed slowly, overall conditioning is improved by moving quickly from exercise to exercise. Start with the largest muscle groups and proceed to the smallest. The larger the muscle worked, the harder the exercise. Push those large muscular structures (hips and thighs) when you are most fresh. Once you are familiar with the equipment and the routine, the entire workout, lifting and lowering the weights in a controlled manner and moving from machine to machine quickly should take no more than 30 minutes. In this manner, you are working your musculoskeletal system (muscle-bones) as well as your cardio-respiratory system (heart-lungs) in the most efficient manner possible. If you work each muscle group thoroughly and intensely, you will elevate your heart rate on your first exercise and by moving quickly from machine to machine, keep your heart rate elevated for the remainder of your workout. This type of workout is the finest workout a healthy trainee can perform. Make every repetition of every exercise a quality repetition and move quickly between exercises. A careful break-in (incorporating short rest periods between exercises) into this type of training is recommended for several weeks once a commitment to sensible, structured exercise is begun.

Get Stronger

This translates into an aesthetically firmer body along with stronger soft tissues and harder bones. The stronger you are, the better you move and the less prone you are to injury. While you cannot lessen the forces in life that you are subjected to daily, you can improve your structural integrity to withstand those forces. In order to get firmer, you must get stronger. Women will not develop large muscles from increasing resistance on the machines, but their muscles and bones *will* get harder. As men get stronger, they will increase muscular size according to the limits of their genetic potential. Building large muscles is extremely difficult for men who want them, let alone women who do not.

Use the Machines

If full range exercise - working a muscle throughout its full range of function from extension to full muscular contraction with proper variable resistance is important to you (as it must be) then truly scientific exercise machines are your obvious choice. Although a barbell, used correctly, is a productive tool, a properly built machine will do everything a barbell will and much more in a safer, more efficient manner. A muscle shortens its length when contracting. In order to involve all available muscular fibers, there must be resistance in the position of full muscular contraction. There is no muscular resistance in the contracted position of most barbell exercises.

Keep It Brief

Meaningful workouts, exercises that stimulate a response from the overall system, inevitably take a toll on the system's recovery ability. Long, drawn out workouts or too many workouts per week may drain the system extensively, not allowing sufficient recovery. One hard set of each exercise stimulates results. Two or three sets of the same exercise (if worked intensely) is always a step backwards; leads to overtraining, substituting more work for harder work, lengthening the workout and lowering the intensity. If you are not constantly getting stronger, increasing your weights, chances are that you are performing too much exercise, too often. Brief, intense exercise stimulates response, rest allows that response. Though individual muscles may recover quickly from hard training sessions, there is a deep inroad into the overall recovery system. The system will not recover so quickly and may take several days or more to completely recover. The body responds best when trained as a unit. (As it rests or feeds as a unit.) Thus, the so-called split routine system of training different body parts on different days is usually a mistake; will again lead to overtraining instead of brief high intensity exercise. The truth is that the stronger the trainee, the more intensely she or he trains, the _less_ hard exercise he or she will be able to tolerate.

Muscle magazines often outline a greater number of sets for exercising one muscle group than I include in my entire workout. When you perform multiple sets of the same exercise, you are merely working the same fibers over and over. Working muscles from many different angles is muscle magazine talk – enticing readers to somehow sculpt and shape their muscles. Baloney! Only by raising your intensity level, rather than the quantity of work, will you recruit new fibers which is what must happen to stimulate muscular strength. You accomplish that with a single high intensity set per exercise.

Train to Failure

Failure in strength training is the inability to perform another repetition in good form. Most trainees believe that the hard repetitions at the end of a set are somehow dangerous, to be avoided. The fact is that every repetition of an exercise is a warm-up leading to the last repetition. Injuries occur in strength training by moving the resistance too fast in the early repetitions of an exercise when the trainee is stronger and can generate the most force.

Resistance in most cases should be low enough to permit at least 8 full range repetitions of an exercise but high enough to prevent more than 12. By the final repetition, force production is lower and you are barely capable of moving a weight which was easier on your first several repetitions. The last repetition is the most important. Leaving out those hard reps greatly reduces the potential benefit of exercise. When you can perform the top number of repetitions (proper form, failure on the last), increase resistance by about 5 percent.

One Set To Failure

One set to failure is the way to go – both physiologically <u>and</u> psychologically. Picture yourself in the middle of a hard set of leg presses. You are working the large musculature of your gluteals, hamstrings and quadriceps. You barely made 11 reps in your previous workout and you know it will be tough to better that today. But you are breathing hard, focused and strong. You have a mindset to succeed; and you do – 12 reps – a new record!

A second, less productive scenario has you on that same leg press, training hard. You have been told (elsewhere) that 3 sets would stimulate greater results. Breathing like a freight train, aching in your hips and legs, you subliminally focus on your 2nd and 3rd set of leg presses and cut your first set short of failure. You don't do those tough reps because you realize you have two more sets left. Big mistake <u>and</u> join the club. This is what most of the other trainees out there are doing. Spinning their wheels, confused with quantity vs. quality!

Move every repetition slowly, when you cannot do another repetition, try it anyway. For example, if your goal is 12 repetitions and you succeed, go for your 13th, 14th or more until you fail to complete a repetition in perfect form. Breathe with your mouth open, do not hold your breath. This level of fatigue coupled with a sufficient period of rest following the workout will stimulate an increase in strength.

Keeping the reps slightly higher in the leg press (10-15) ensures a greater measure of safety as the leg press (or squat) calls the vulnerable knees and lower back into action. For this reason, my program pre-exhausts the legs and hips and schedules the leg press at the end of the lower body sequence. At that point, the large hip and leg muscles are fatigued, so the weight in the leg press is necessarily lower than it would be if the involved musculature was fresh.

Forget the oft-quoted mistaken belief that very high repetitions increase muscular definition. You now know that it is your amount of body fat that determines definition. Harder muscles and less fat = more definition.

Very high repetitions and light resistance, as recommended by most women's fashion magazines, deteriorates into nothing more than aerobic exercise, and your muscles and bones after some initial stimulation will gain little if any strength. High intensity strength training performed as it should be, as it is taught in this book, will always be the exercise of choice - at least for those people seeking the most sensible way to improve functional ability and everyday life.

Pre-Exhaustion

This is the process of isolating (as nearly as possible) a muscle during an exercise and then taking it past its point of failure by immediately following the isolation exercise with a compound movement that brings in other muscular groups but still works the muscle exhausted by the previous isolation exercise.

What Is Pre-Exhaustion?

Pre-exhaustion, isolating a muscular structure with a single joint movement and immediately following with a multiple joint (compound) movement, is probably the best way to exercise a muscle and certainly the safest. Pre-exhaustion can be used for virtually every muscular structure in many combinations.

EXAMPLES

EXERCISE	MUSCLE GROUP(S)
1. Leg Extension	Quadriceps
2. Squat	Gluteals, Hamstrings, Quadriceps
1. Leg Curl	Hamstrings
2. Leg Press	Gluteals, Hamstrings, Quadriceps
1. Pullover	Torso Musculature
2. Torso Arm, Row, Chins	Biceps, Torso Musculature
1. Arm Cross	Pectorals
2. Chest Press, Dips	Triceps, Pectorals, Deltoids
1. Lateral Raise	Deltoids
2. Overhead Press, Dips	Triceps, Deltoids, Pectorals
1. Bicep Curl	Biceps
2. Torso Arm, Row, Chins	Biceps, Torso Musculature
1. Tricep Extension	Triceps
2. Dip or Any Press	Triceps, Pectorals, Deltoids

Barbell Squat vs. MedX Leg Press

The full squat is the most productive of all free weight exercises when performed correctly as shown – full, deep controlled repetitions. Squats work the largest muscular structures of the body, namely the gluteals and thighs. However, the potential orthopedic cost to the cervical and lumbar spine, and in some cases the knees, will for many women exceed the strength and conditioning benefits.

Editor's Note: In 1964 at a Penn State University Powerlifting Competition, I successfully squatted with 424 lbs. at a bodyweight of 180.5 pounds. This was a full squat, hips far below parallel with a definite pause in the bottom position. X-rays taken two years later relative to recurrent low back pain revealed significant skeletal damage, no doubt in part due to my misuse of a barbell. Structural damage – degenerative change at twenty one years old!

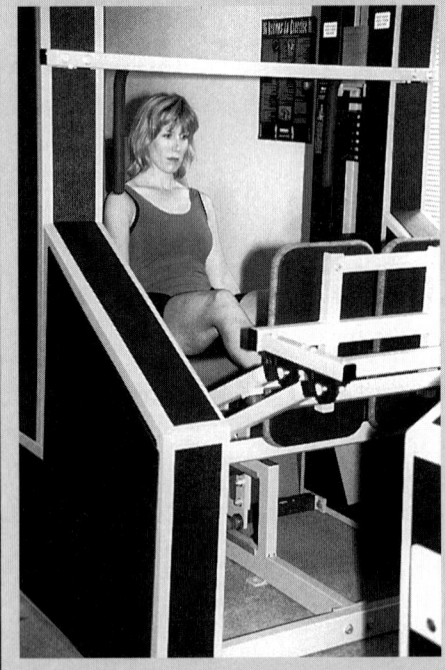

Barbell Squat vs. MedX Leg Press

The MedX leg press, though allowing less range of movement than the barbell squat, is in many cases a safer alternative to the full squat. Performed intensely, it will approximate the stimulus of the squat without spinal compression and the need for "spotters" to monitor the lift.

For example, the exercise called the leg extension works the quadriceps which extends the frontal thigh. When the leg press immediately follows, the gluteal muscles come into play to take the still working quadriceps past failure. The leg press is a compound exercise because it rotates around more than one joint. (This principle works equally well when the leg curl, which contracts the rear thigh, precedes the leg press). These exercises will be detailed in the next chapter.

> **Maximize Results**
>
> Both the squat and leg press are very demanding exercises that when performed correctly are capable of stimulating a tremendous response in overall strength and cardio-respiratory conditioning. The safest, most productive way to utilize either the squat or leg press in the workout is through the "pre-exhaustion" principle.

Pre- exhaustion has been ignored by most of the strength training community, but it is one of the staples of a safe, sensible workout.

Workout Frequency

In order to reach your maximum potential, you should never workout more than twice a week. For example, strength training exercise should be performed on Monday and Thursday, Tuesday and Friday or Wednesday and Saturday. Always allow adequate rest between workouts. Remember, exercise stimulates the body to respond. Rest allows the response.

The Workout Journal

Carrying a workout journal where you can record your workout routine will help keep you focused. Before each workout write down the exercise and the resistance to be used. Following the workouts record the repetitions performed. Once you are able to perform 12 or more reps for a particular exercise, increase the resistance the next workout. The exception is the leg press which you should be able to perform 15 reps before increasing the resistance.

EXAMPLE

MONDAY

Exercise	Resistance(*)	Repetitions
Hip Extension	(180)	11
Leg Extension	(174)	**12**
Leg Curl	(170)	10
Leg Press	(480)	**16**
Pullover	(70)	11
Torso-Arm	(180)	8
Lateral Raise	(56)	10
Overhead Press	(110)	9
Assisted Chin-ups (optional)	(50)	10
Assisted Dips (optional)	(50)	11
Torso Flexion	(70)	**12**

THURSDAY

Exercise	Resistance(*)	Repetitions
Hip Extension	(180)	**12**
Leg Extension	(180)	10
Leg Curl	(170)	11
Leg Press	(496)	11
Abduction (optional)	(88)	10
Adduction (optional)	(120)	10
Pullover	(70)	**12**
Rowing	(170)	10
Arm Cross	(70)	11
Chest Press	(86)	9
Torso Flexion	(74)	10

(*) Exercise poundage will vary depending on the equipment manufacturer and the cams and length of levers used on separate pieces of equipment. Exercises in this book were performed primarily on Med X machines.

Record Keeping

Very Important! People who do not keep a journal tend to get lost and will do extra sets of exercises under the misguided assumption that they are doing harder work when, in reality, they are just doing more work. Meaningful exercise is "double-progressive" – an increase in weight handled and/or number of repetitions from one workout to the next (with proper form) reflects progress, and this should be recorded on paper. Record your results in your journal when the entire workout is finished. (You will remember – there are not that many exercises.) Rest for a few days, return to action and, when goals are met, increase your resistance and/or reps.

Stay Focused

Perform each exercise as if it is the final exercise in your routine. Do not pace yourself in order to complete the ten or twelve exercise program. Greater results will be stimulated going all out on fewer exercises than holding back to finish the intended workout. Through the years, I have seen many lean, strong women who performed only a total of eight exercises and *never* included either abductor-adductor or chins and dips (or biceps and triceps) in any of their workouts. The basic routine without these exercises was more than enough to stimulate the desired results. Remember, the amount of exercise can be sacrificed, the level of intensity cannot.

Even The "Ideal" May Be Too Much

Though this book hammers away at twice a week workouts, this, too, is not "etched in stone" or the "final word." Recovery varies among intense training women. Three times every two weeks (i.e. Monday, Friday and the following Wednesday) or even one workout per week has empirically yielded outstanding strength gains. Keep an accurate workout journal. If you are not making steady progress, question your intensity or the frequency or length of your workouts. Searching for easier training methods and/or greater volume or frequency is never the solution.

A Final Word on Athletes – Diminishing Returns

Some sports provide a significant aerobic workout in practice and in the game itself. The athlete should have the leeway to find the right mix of strength training and aerobics for herself, but for most, a properly designed and executed strength workout combines the best of both worlds. In any event, both coach and athlete must beware of the dangers of diminishing returns and orthopedic risk.

Young female athletes competing today in sports such as gymnastics, swimming and rowing are often confronted with suffocating schedules. They get up early, practice, rush through breakfast, go to school, practice again, have a fast-food dinner ... then the cycle resumes the next day. This can lead quickly to physiological and psychological burnout, and we are seeing more and more female athletes drop out when they reach their mid-teens – including Olympic gymnasts and swimmers. At all levels, the pressure of training, practice and competition can drain the athlete physically and emotionally, as she tries to balance the demands of her sport, school, family and social life. Many reach a point where their body rebels and they wind up in sick bay.

If the burnout is not terminal, however, a

revelation may follow. The layoff recharges her batteries. After a prolonged absence, she returns to action and turns in her best time (or performance) ever. Her coach says, "Imagine what she would have done if she had not been sick." The truth is that she did as well as she did because she had been forced to take time off. The moral of the story: too much training, too much pressure, too little rest are counter-productive.

Rest And Reap The Rewards

Proper exercise stimulates the body to respond. Rest allows that response. This is the essence of the "cause and effect" of exercise stressed throughout this book which you will rarely see elsewhere in print.

11. Sample Workouts

The principles discussed in the last chapter are embodied in the following full-body workouts which emphasize variable-resistance, full range of motion weight-training machines. These principles apply to whatever equipment is available to you.

Workout 1
1. Hip Extension
2. Leg Extension
3. Leg Curl
4. Leg Press
5. Hip Abduction
6. Hip Adduction
7. Pullover
8. Torso-Arm or Rowing
9. Arm Cross
10. Any Chest Press
11. Torso Flexion or Abdominal
12. Lumbar Extension

Workout 2
1. Hip Extension
2. Leg Extension
3. Leg Curl
4. Leg Press
5. Pullover
6. Torso-Arm or Rowing
7. Lateral Raise
8. Overhead Press
9. Bicep Curl or Assisted Chin-Ups
10. Tricep Extension or Assisted Dips or SeatedDips
11. Torso Flexion or Abdominal
12. Cervical Extension

Free Weights
1. Barbell Squat
2. Chin-Ups
3. Overhead Press
4. Bent-over Row
5. Bench Press
6. Barbell Curl
7. Parallel Dips
8. Barbell Dead Lift

Workout 1

(Exercises in Sequence)
(*) Indicates full range of motion exercise.

Lower Body

Exercise	Muscle Group(s)
1. Hip Extension (*) (8-12 reps):	gluteals hamstrings quadriceps lower back
2. Leg Extension (*) (8-12 reps):	quadriceps
3. Leg Curl (*) (8-12 reps):	hamstrings
4. Leg Press (12-15 reps):	gluteals hamstrings quadriceps
5. Hip Abduction (optional) (*) (8-12 reps):	outer hip
6. Hip Adduction (optional) (*) (8-12 reps):	inner thigh

Upper Body

Exercise	Muscle Group(s)
7. Pullover (*) (8-12 reps):	torso musculature trapezius abdominals
8. Torso-Arm or Rowing (8-12 reps):	biceps torso musculature
9. Arm Cross (*) (8-12 reps):	pectorals deltoids
10. Any Chest Press (8-12 reps):	triceps pectorals deltoids
11. Torso Flexion or Abdominal (*) (8-12 reps):	hip flexors abdominals
12. Lumbar Extension (*) (8-12 reps):	lumbar extensors

WORKOUT 1:
Exercise #1. Hip Extension (*)

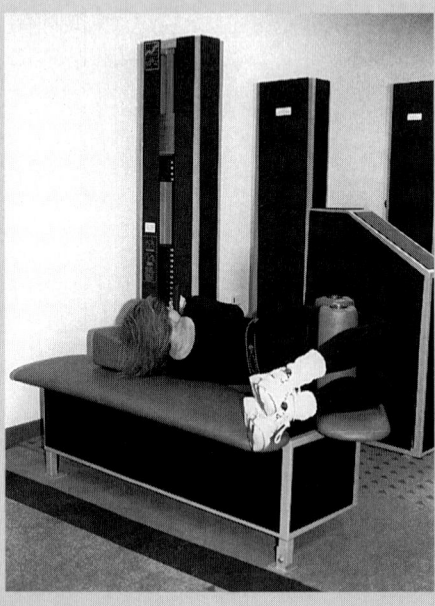

This exercise revolves around the single axis of the hip joint and draws the legs in line with the torso. Lying on your side, you work the muscles from a stretched position to a position of full muscular contraction with balanced variable resistance throughout the range of motion.

This is a single joint movement that concentrates on the gluteal muscles, but also brings the hamstrings and the muscles of the lower back into play.

WORKOUT 1:
Exercise #2. Leg Extension (*)

The leg extension is a single joint movement around the axis of the knee that is not worked full-range in the stretch position because to do so would potentially exert too much force on what is the largest but most inefficient joint in the body (the knee). Actual movement on the MedX Leg Extension encompasses about 110 degrees out of a possible 130-140 degrees, but this is still the most direct and safest exercise for the body's second largest muscle group, the quadriceps (frontal thigh muscles), which extend the lower leg.

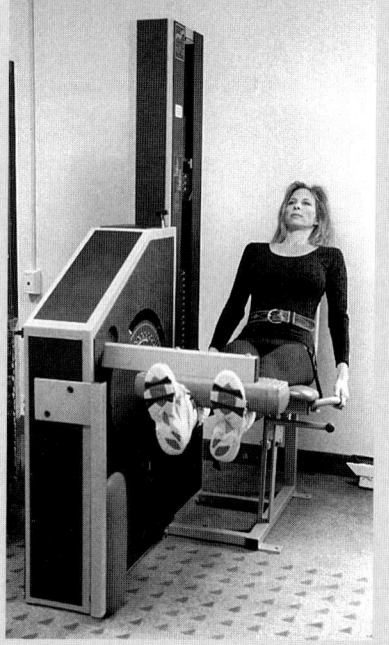

WORKOUT 1:
Exercise #3. Leg Curl (*)

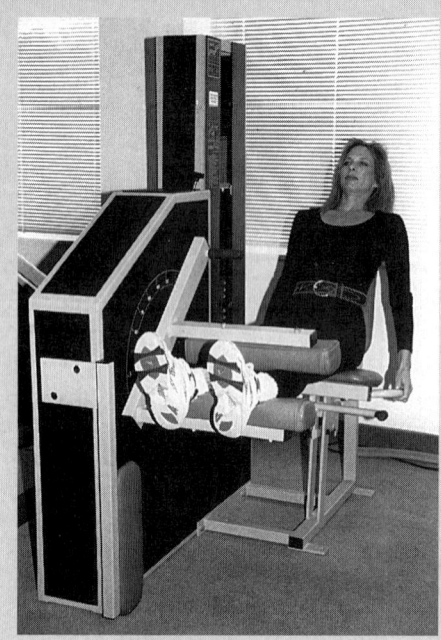

This exercise can be performed on your side, or in the seated or prone positions depending on available equipment. The exercise works the hamstrings by bending the lower legs back toward the buttocks. As in Exercise #2, the only axis of rotation is around the knee joint. Since there are always two muscles around a joint, any exercise targeting one automatically involves the other. In Exercise #2, as you contract the quadriceps, you are stretching the hamstrings. In Exercise #3, you stretch the quadriceps as you contract the hamstrings.

WORKOUT 1:
Prone Leg Curl (*) – Variation of Exercise #3

The prone leg curl is a variation of the seated leg curl (Exercise #3). The same muscles are worked, only in a different position.

WORKOUT 1:
Exercise #4. Leg Press

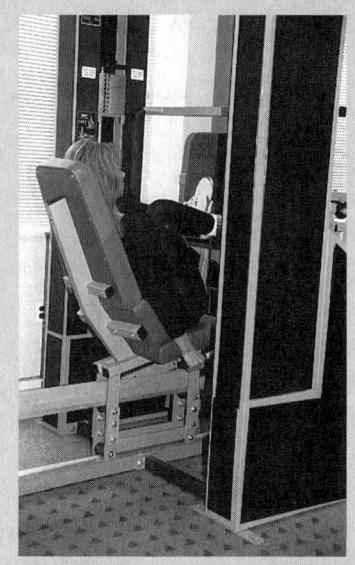

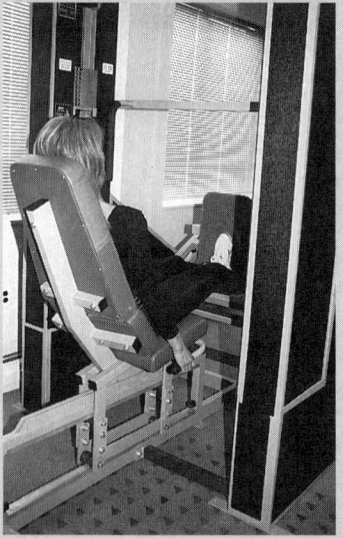

This exercise involves the muscles already worked in the first three exercises and is, consequently, not a full-range exercise but a compound movement that includes more than one joint and works a large muscle mass. Also, the calf muscles, which haven't been worked previously in the workout, indirectly come into play here.

In this instance, the price you pay for bringing in other muscle groups is that you are no longer doing full-range exercise; there is little resistance in the locked-out position because the bones have taken over at that point; the muscles are worked in linear rather than rotary fashion. But by combining previously worked muscle groups with fresh muscles, you can take the fatigued muscles beyond the failure threshold (see *Pre-exhaustion* in Chapter 10).

Since the gluteals, quadriceps, and hamstrings have been fatigued by the previous exercises, you will not be moving as great a weight as you would have if your muscles were fresh. The resulting necessity for a lighter resistance is a built-in safety measure, since the leg press (or squat) inherently places some compressive forces on both the lumbar spine and the knee. The order of exercises recommended here allows a productive routine without structural compromise.

WORKOUT 1:
Exercise #5. Hip Abduction (*)

Rotating solely about the hip joint, this exercise works the muscles of the outer hips and thighs.

WORKOUT 1:
Exercise #6. Hip Adduction (*)

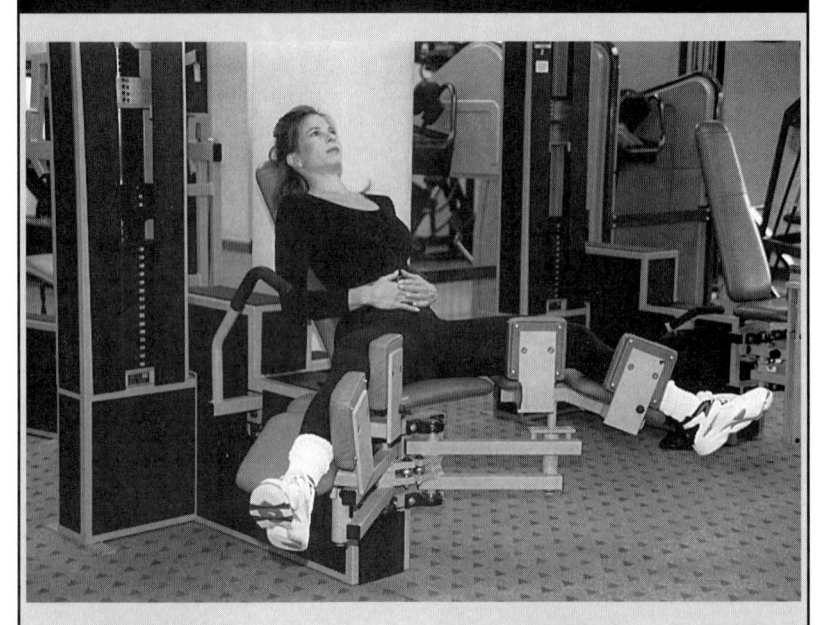

A mirror image of Exercise #5, this movement works the muscles of the inner thighs.

WORKOUT 1:
Exercise #7. Pullover (*)

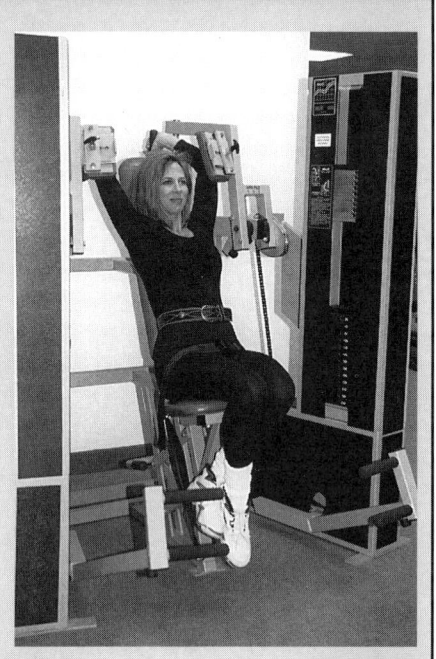

This movement potentially rotates over 200 degrees around the shoulder joint and provides a high order of work for the latissimus, pectorals, trapezius and other muscles of the torso. It also thoroughly involves the abdominal muscles, but is designed so that the arm muscles have little interplay. Arthur Jones has accurately referred to this machine as the "Upper Body Squat" because it effectively works so much of the torso musculature.

The movement parallels one function of the latissimus – namely, to move the humerus down and past the torso. At this point in the workout, if you have been exercising to failure, using proper form, and moving quickly from machine to machine, you are well into receiving a pronounced aerobic effect as well as stimulating muscular strength.

WORKOUT 1:
Exercise #8. Rowing

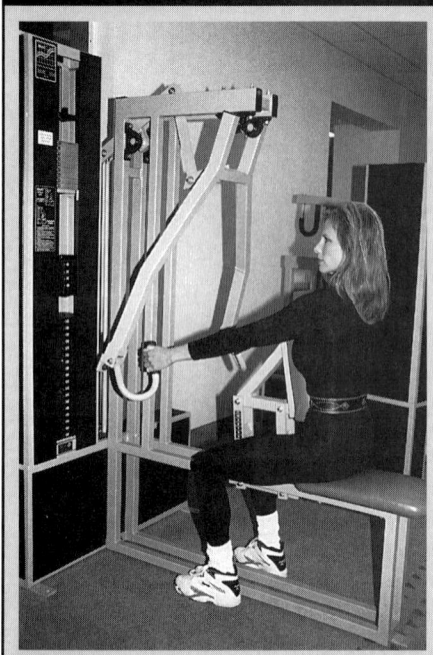

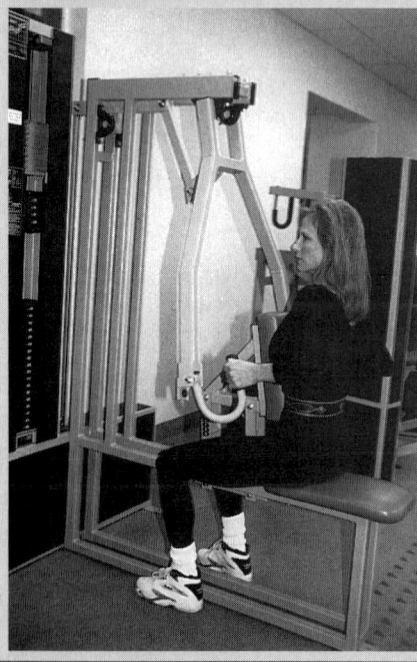

This is a compound movement rotating around the elbows and shoulders. It is another exercise for the torso, but it brings in the fresh biceps to take the exhausted torso muscles past failure. For just a few seconds, the smaller, weaker muscles of the arms are actually stronger than the exhausted latissimus, so if you seize the moment, you can take the latissimus muscles into a deeper state of fatigue. In this fashion, these exhausted muscles receive a safe, beneficial increment of work that they cannot obtain by simply doing another set of the primary exercise (in this case, Exercise #7). To take advantage of this window of opportunity, you must move from one machine to the next without rest.

WORKOUT 1:
Torso-Arm – Variation of Exercise #8

The Torso-Arm exercise is an alternative to the rowing exercise.

WORKOUT 1:
Exercise #9. Arm Cross (*)

This is a single joint movement for the pectoral muscles and the related deltoid structures, paralleling their function of drawing the humerus down and across the chest. Rotation is around the shoulder joint, and the arm muscles are not involved in the exercise.

WORKOUT 1:
Exercise #10. Chest Press

After isolating as nearly as possible the muscle groups in Exercise #9, bringing in the fresh triceps will push those fatigued pectorals to a more intense level, much like the biceps do for the torso in Exercise #8.

WORKOUT 1:
Exercise #11. Torso Flexion (*)

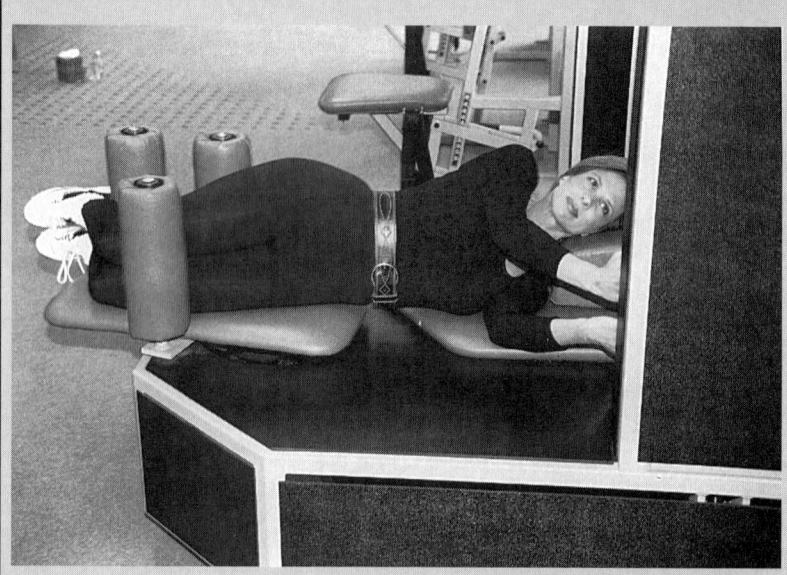

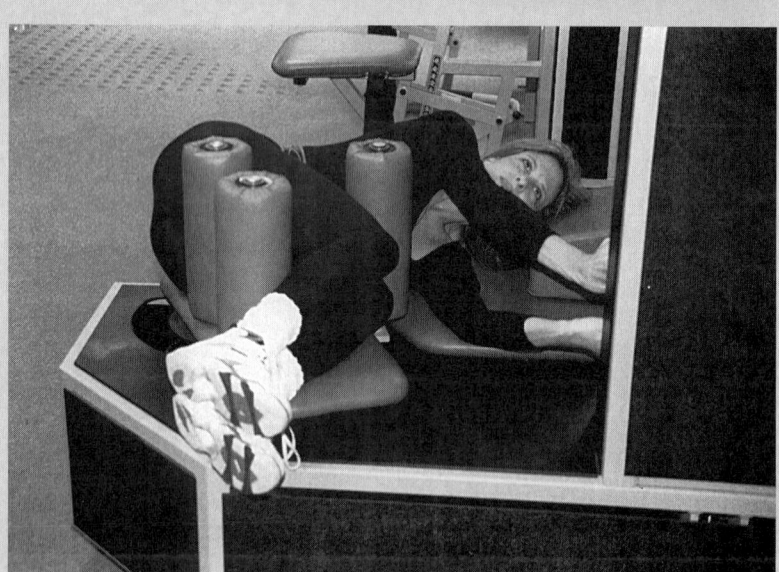

Lying on your side, you perform a single-axis movement that concentrates on the hip flexors and the abdominals.

WORKOUT 1:
Abdominal (*) – Variation of Exercise #11

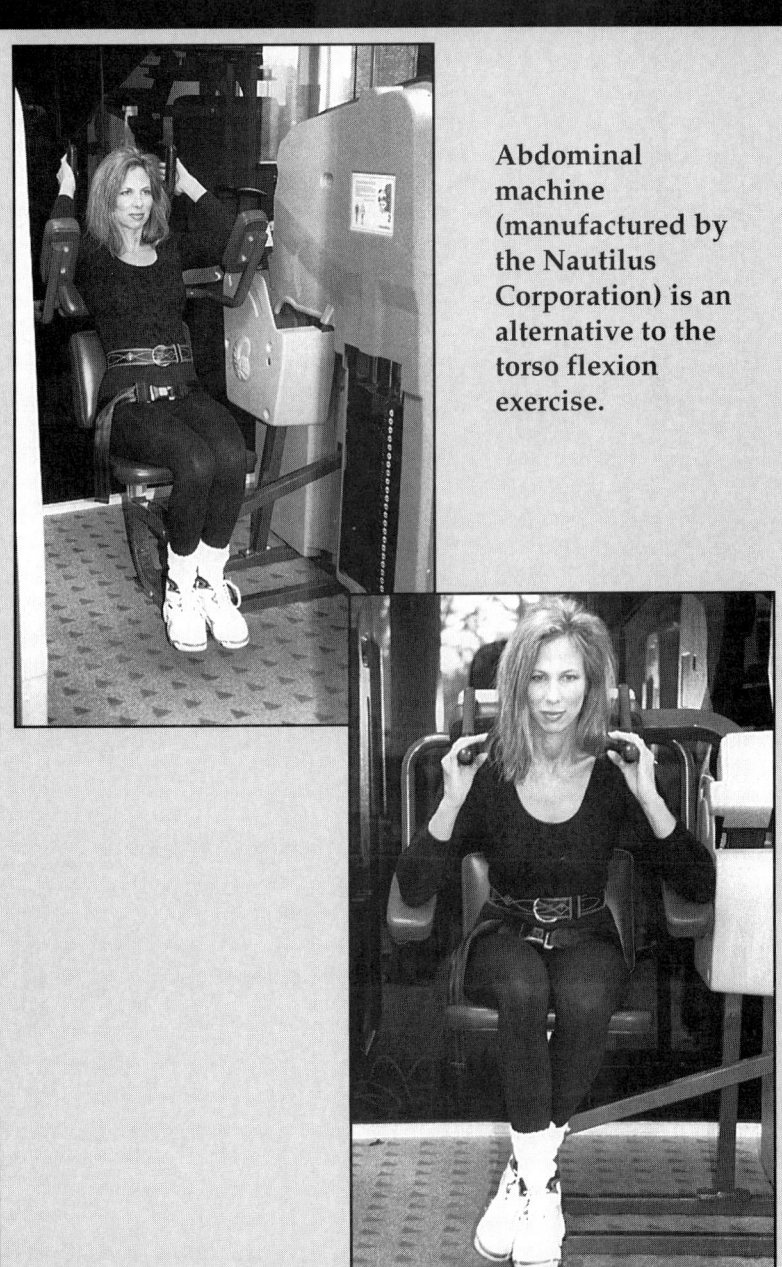

Abdominal machine (manufactured by the Nautilus Corporation) is an alternative to the torso flexion exercise.

WORKOUT 1:
Exercise #12. Lumbar Extension (*)

Unless the pelvis is anchored, the muscles that extend the lumbar spine are impossible to isolate. In most exercises geared to reach the lumbar area, the pelvis is free to move and thus the gluteal and hamstring muscles provide most of the force while the lumbar muscles go along for the ride. The MedX Lumbar Extension machine anchors the pelvis and isolates the lumbar extensor muscles.

The lower back with its joints, ligaments and disks is a masterpiece of design, but the origin of most back problems is an inherent weakness of the muscles that extend the lumbar spine. You can be strong in the hips without corresponding strength in the lower back, putting yourself at orthopedic risk.

The same machine can be utilized to provide rehabilitative exercise for this very vulnerable area of the body. (Refer to #6 in "Additional Workout Notes," the final section in this chapter).

Workout 2

(Exercises in Sequence)
(*) Indicates full range of motion exercise.

Lower Body

Exercise	Muscle Group(s)
1. Hip Extension (*) (8-12 reps):	gluteals hamstrings quadriceps lower back
2. Leg Extension (*) (8-12 reps):	quadriceps
3. Leg Curl (*) (8-12 reps):	hamstrings
4. Leg Press (12-15 reps):	gluteals hamstrings quadriceps

Upper Body

Exercise	Muscle Group(s)
5. Pullover (*) (8-12 reps):	torso musculature trapezius abdominals
6. Torso-Arm or Rowing (8-12 reps):	biceps torso musculature
7. Lateral Raise (*) (8-12 reps):	deltoids
8. Overhead Press (8-12 reps):	triceps deltoids pectorals
9. Bicep Curl (*) or Assisted Chin-Ups (8-12 reps)	biceps biceps torso musculature
10. Tricep Extension (*) or Assisted or Seated Dips (8-12 reps)	triceps triceps, pectorals, deltoids
11. Torso Flexion or Abdominal (*) (8-12 reps):	hip flexors abdominals
12. Cervical Extension (*) (8-12 reps):	cervical extensors

WORKOUT 2:
Exercise #1. Hip Extension (*)

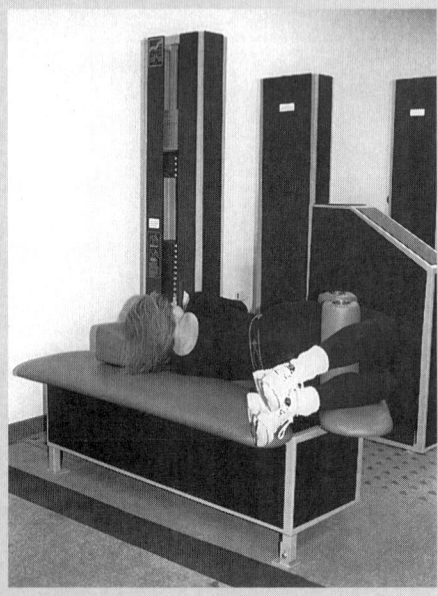

This exercise revolves around the single axis of the hip joint and draws the legs in line with the torso. Lying on your side, you work the muscles from a stretched position to a position of full muscular contraction with balanced variable resistance throughout the range of motion.

This is a single joint movement that concentrates on the gluteal muscles, but also brings the hamstrings and the muscles of the lower back into play.

WORKOUT 2:
Exercise #2. Leg Extension (*)

The leg extension is a single joint movement around the axis of the knee that is not worked full-range in the stretch position because to do so would potentially exert too much force on what is the largest but most inefficient joint in the body (the knee). Actual movement on the MedX Leg Extension encompasses about 110 degrees out of a possible 130-140 degrees, but this is still the most direct and safest exercise for the body's second largest muscle group, the quadriceps (frontal thigh muscles), which extend the lower leg.

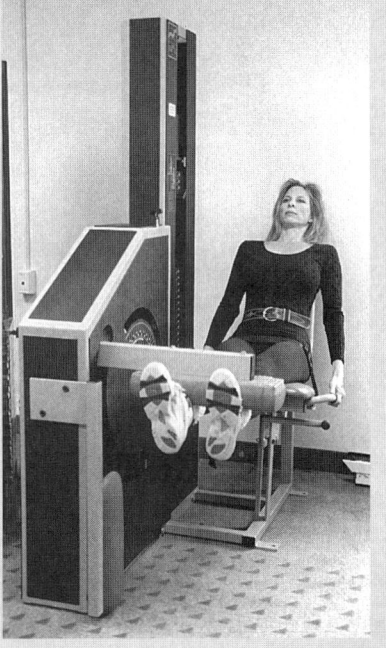

WORKOUT 2:
Exercise #3. Leg Curl (*)

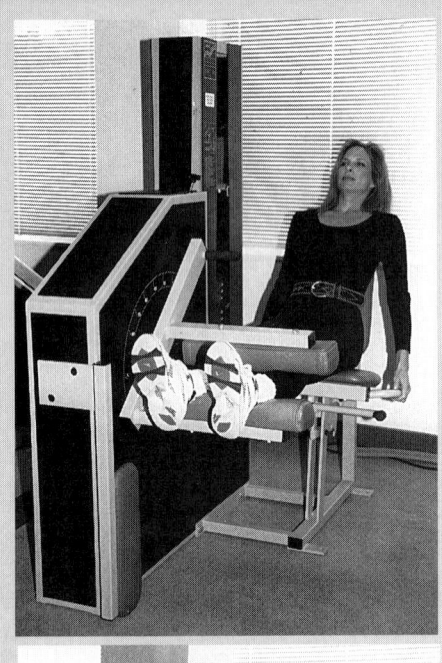

This exercise can be performed on your side, or in the seated or prone positions depending on available equipment. The exercise works the hamstrings by bending the lower legs back toward the buttocks. As in Exercise #2, the only axis of rotation is around the knee joint. Since there are always two muscles around a joint, any exercise targeting one automatically involves the other. In Exercise #2, as you contract the quadriceps, you are stretching the hamstrings. In Exercise #3, you stretch the quadriceps as you contract the hamstrings.

WORKOUT 2:
Prone Leg Curl (*) – Variation of Exercise #3

The prone leg curl is a variation of the seated leg curl (Exercise #3). The same muscles are worked, only in a different position.

WORKOUT 2:
Exercise #4. Leg Press

This exercise involves the muscles already worked in the first three exercises and is, consequently, not a full-range exercise but a compound movement that includes more than one joint and works a large muscle mass. Also, the calf muscles, which haven't been worked previously in the workout, indirectly come into play here.

In this instance, the price you pay for bringing in other muscle groups is that you are no longer doing full-range exercise; there is little resistance in the locked-out position because the bones have taken over at that point; the muscles are worked in linear rather than rotary fashion. But by combining previously worked muscle groups with fresh muscles, you can take the fatigued muscles beyond the failure threshold (see *Pre-exhaustion* in Chapter 10).

Since the gluteals, quadriceps, and hamstrings have been fatigued by the previous exercises, you will not be moving as great a weight as you would have if your muscles were fresh. The resulting necessity for a lighter resistance is a built-in safety measure, since the leg press (or squat) inherently places some compressive forces on both the lumbar spine and the knee. The order of exercises recommended here allows a productive routine without structural compromise.

WORKOUT 2:
Exercise #5. Pullover (*)

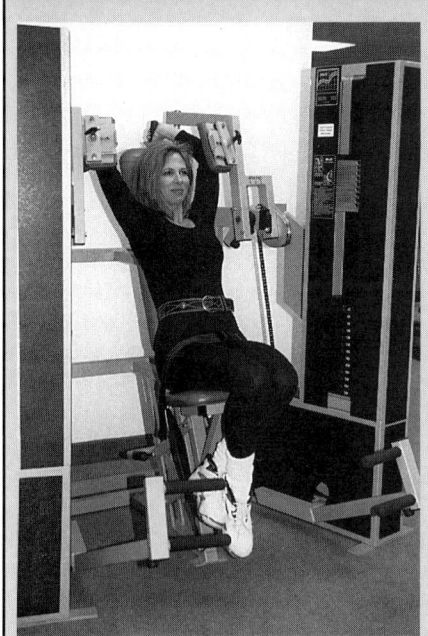

This movement potentially rotates over 200 degrees around the shoulder joint and provides a high order of work for the latissimus, pectorals, trapezius and other muscles of the torso. It also thoroughly involves the abdominal muscles, but is designed so that the arm muscles have little interplay. Arthur Jones has accurately referred to this machine as the "Upper Body Squat" because it effectively works so much of the torso muscles.

The movement parallels one function of the latissimus – namely, to move the humerus down and past the torso. At this point in the workout, if you have been exercising to failure, using proper form, and moving quickly from machine to machine, you are already receiving a pronounced aerobic effect as well as stimulating muscular strength.

WORKOUT 2:
Exercise #6. Rowing

This is a compound movement rotating around the elbows and shoulders. It is another exercise for the torso, but it brings in the fresh biceps to take the exhausted torso muscles past failure. For just a few seconds, the smaller, weaker muscles of the arms are actually stronger than the exhausted latissimus, so if you seize the moment, you can take the latissimus muscles into a deeper state of fatigue. In this fashion, these exhausted muscles receive a safe, beneficial increment of work that they cannot obtain by simply doing another set of the primary exercise (in this case, Exercise #7). To take advantage of this window of opportunity, you must move from one machine to the next without rest.

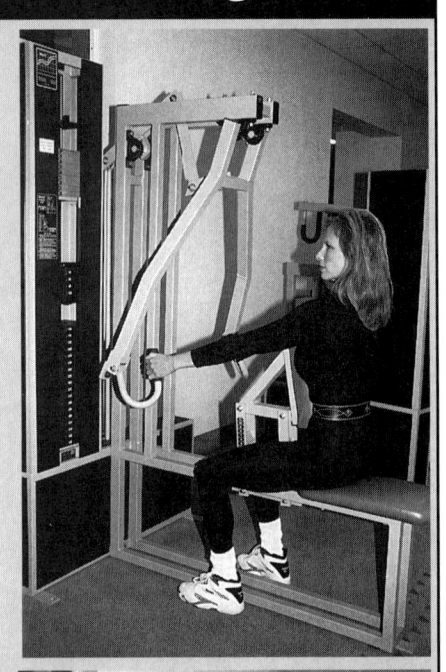

WORKOUT 2:
Torso-Arm – Variation of Exercise #6

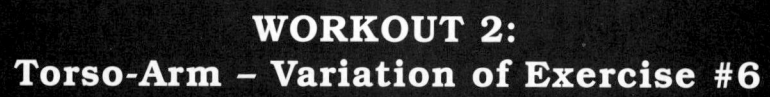

The Torso-Arm exercise is an alternative to the rowing exercise.

WORKOUT 2:
Exercise #7. Lateral Raise (*)

This is a single joint movement for the deltoid muscles which abduct (move out to the side and up) the humerus. The exercise parallels that function.

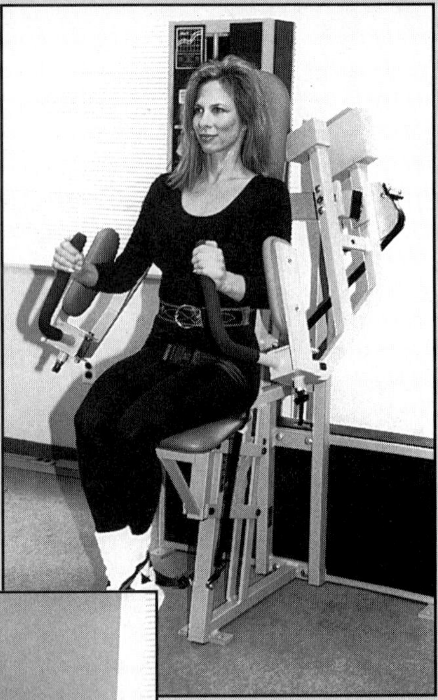

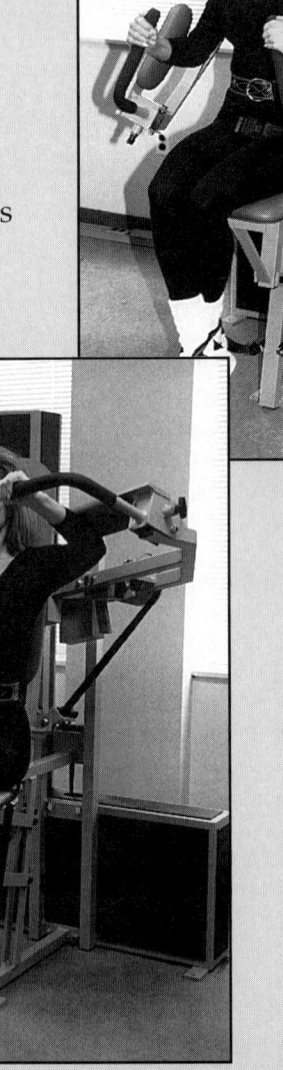

WORKOUT 2:
Exercise #8. Overhead Press

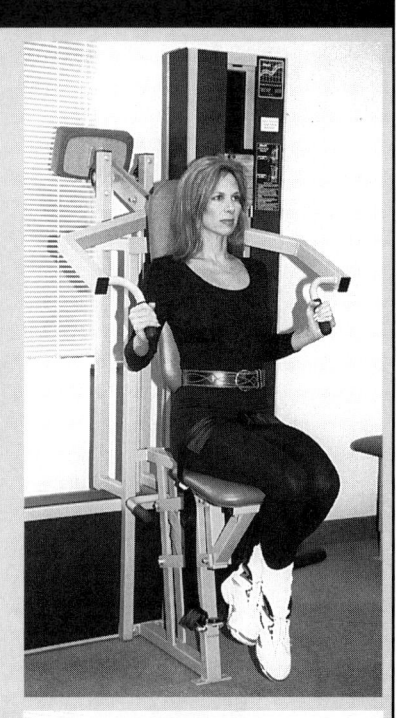

This is a compound exercise that works the upper arms as well as the shoulders. The principle of Pre-Exhaustion is again at work here as the fresh triceps bolster the exhausted deltoids. Since the muscular structures of the chest and shoulders are closely related, it is best to do these last two exercises (#7 and #8) during a session that does not contain exercises #9 and #10 from Sample Workout 1. To do both pairs in the same workout may lead to overtraining.

The shoulder joint is a relatively inefficient ball-and-socket joint, and even if you train correctly, there is a risk of overuse. Overtraining the shoulder with many various pressing movements is a risk that should be acknowledged and avoided in structuring a safe, meaningful workout.

WORKOUT 2:
Exercise #9. Bicep Curl (*)

The bicep curl machine provides direct work for the biceps.

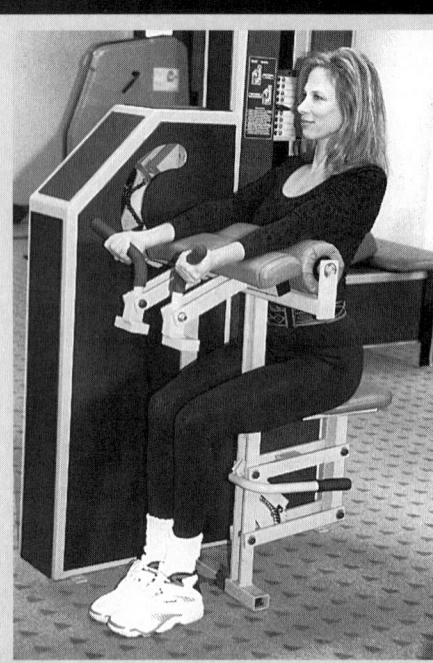

WORKOUT 2:
Assisted Chin-Ups – Variation of Exercise #9

*G*ravitron, the assisted chin-up machine manufactured by Stairmaster Sports/Medical, works both the biceps and the torso muscles. The assisted chin machine can be substituted for the bicep curl machine.

WORKOUT 2:
Exercise #10. Tricep Extension (*)

The tricep extension provides direct work for the triceps.

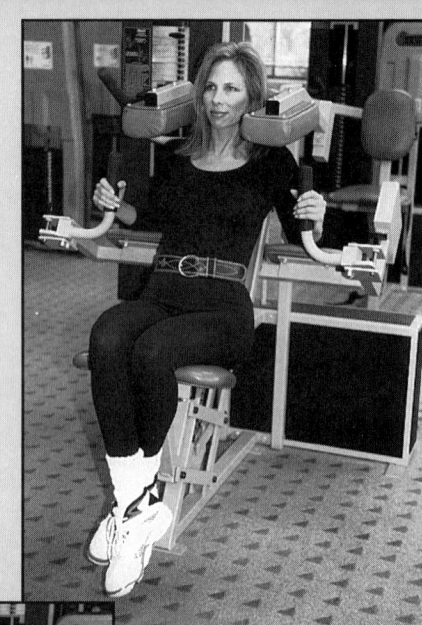

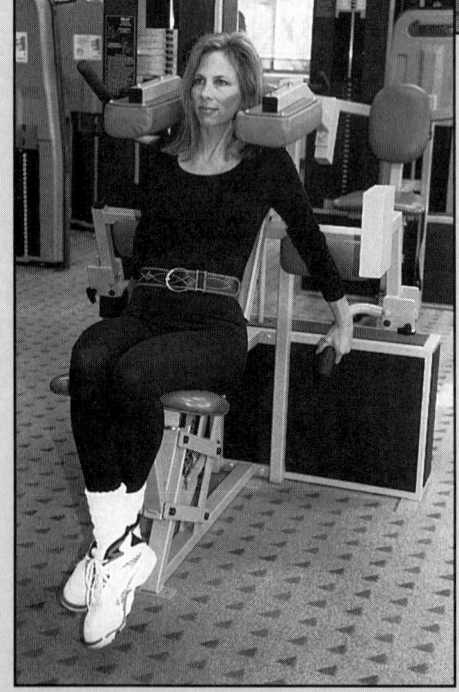

WORKOUT 2:
Assisted Dips – Variation of Exercise #10

Gravitron, the assisted dip machine manufactured by Stairmaster Sports/Medical, works both the triceps and torso muscles. The assisted dip machine can be used as a substitute for the tricep extension machine.

WORKOUT 2:
Seated Dips – Variation of Exercise #10

The seated dip exercise can be used as an alternative to the assisted dip or tricep extension exercises.

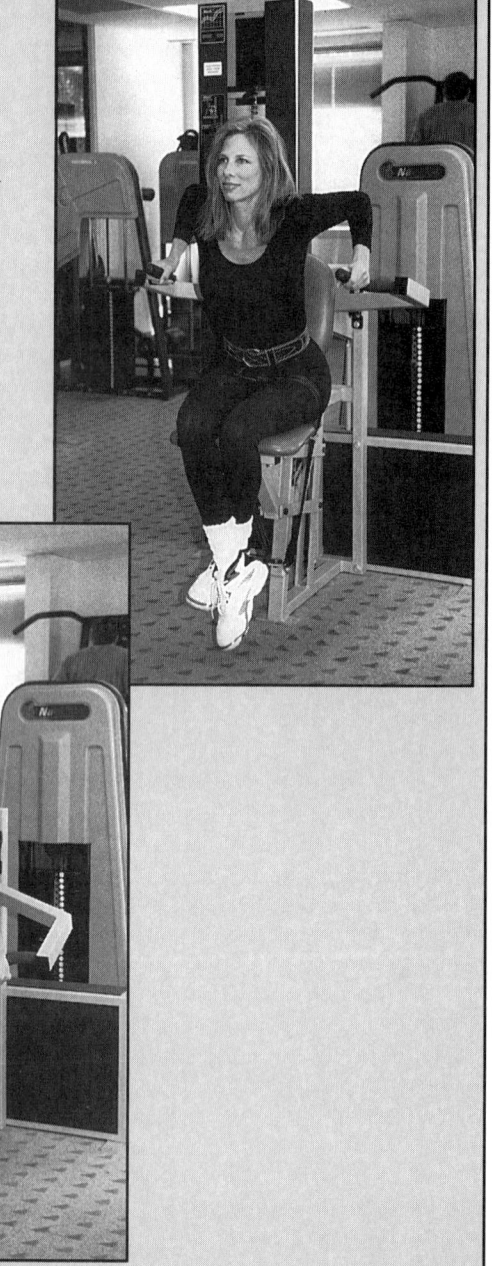

WORKOUT 2:
Exercise #11. Torso Flexion (*)

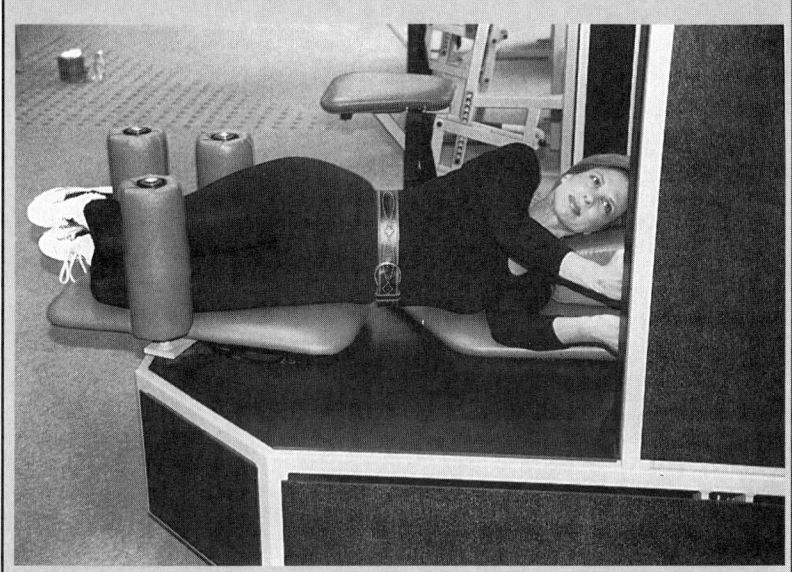

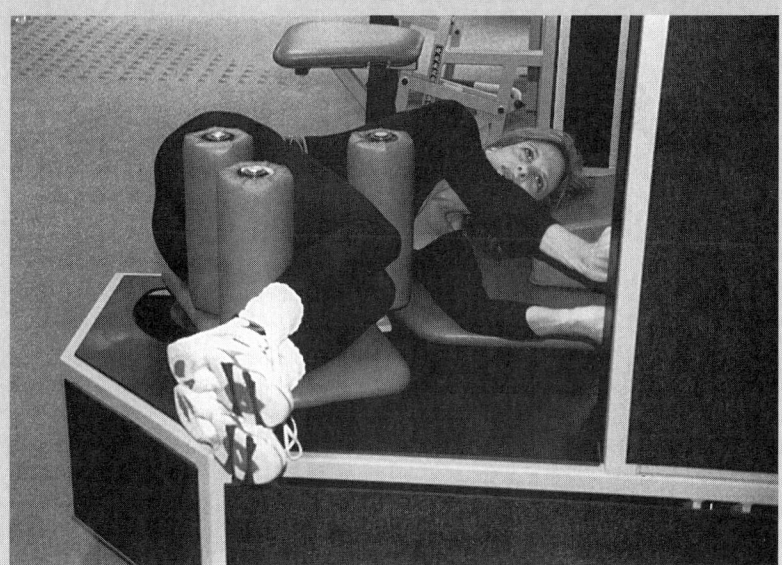

Lying on your side, you perform a single-axis movement that concentrates on the hip flexors and the abdominals.

WORKOUT 2:
Abdominal (*) – Variation of Exercise #11

Abdominal machine (manufactured by the Nautilus Corporation) is an alternative to the torso flexion exercise.

WORKOUT 2:
Exercise #12. Cervical Extension (*)

Another breakthrough in regular training and rehab is the MedX Cervical Extension machine which restricts movement of the torso in order to isolate the muscles that extend the cervical spine (neck area) – another area of the body prone to injury arising from soft-tissue weakness. (Refer to #6 in "Additional Workout Notes," the final section in this chapter).

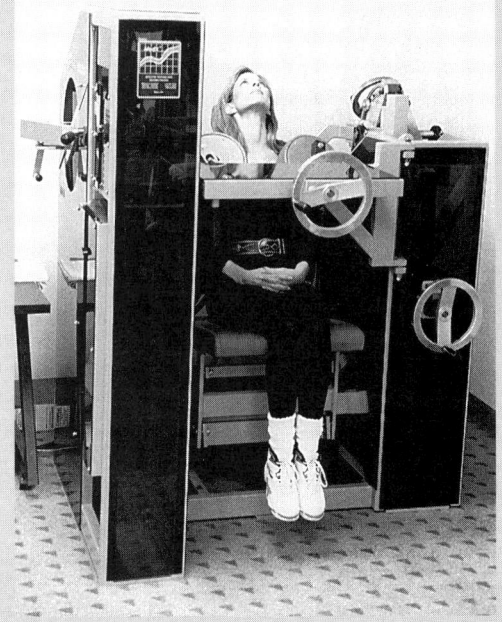

NOTES:

1. Both workouts 1 and 2 work the entire body.

2. The first workout includes direct work for the abductor-adductor (hip/thigh) muscles, while the second does not. The second workout includes chins and dips or direct biceps-triceps work, while the first does not. These exercises are optional.

3. Many women believe they need additional abdominal exercise to burn the fat off their stomachs. However, additional abdominal work is neither necessary nor desirable. The abdominals receive indirect work on nearly all movements in the workout. Remember, fat cannot be "spot-reduced." Excessive abdominal work will not burn additional fatty tissue off the midsection.

4. Slight changes in the order of exercises, and an occasional substitution of exercises, is acceptable. Again, there is no need to anguish over the perfect workout.

5. The small muscle groups of the calf and forearm will respond best when exercised directly. If you wish, you may substitute heel raises periodically for the abductor-adductor and add wrist curls after chins and dips or bicep-tricep pairings. Of course, all of these small muscle groups are always worked at least indirectly within the basic routine.

6. The MedX equipment featured per exercise #12 in each workout is a major breakthrough in the field of sports medicine and is specialized and is not widely available.

NOTES (continued):

The alternates of choice for these two exercises are the Lower-Back and 4-Way Neck machines. However, conventional Lower-Back machines do not eliminate pelvic movement, compromising their ability to isolate the lumbar extensor muscles.

7. If the strength workout is performed with free weights, the intensity level of a free weight workout should be in accordance with the principles outlined throughout this book. The following order of exercises is recommended:

EXERCISE
1. *Barbell Squat (12 -15 reps)*
2. *Chin-ups (8-12 reps)*
3. *Overhead Press (8-12 reps)*
4. *Bent-over Row (8-12 reps)*
5. *Bench Press (8-12 reps)*
6. *Barbell Curl (8-12 reps)*
7. *Parallel Dips (8-12 reps)*
8. *Barbell Dead Lift (12-15 reps)*

8. Although brief, this routine is intense and effective when performed correctly. Small muscle group exercises, such as heel raises for the calves and wrist curls for the forearms, may be added. Safe, direct cervical and lumbar spine work, however, necessitates specialized machines.

Free Weight Sample Workout

Exercise	Muscle Groups
1. Barbell Squat (12 -15 reps):	gluteals hamstrings quadriceps
2. Chin-ups (8-12 reps):	biceps torso musculature
3. Overhead Press (8-12 reps):	triceps deltoids pectorals
4. Bent-over Row (8-12 reps):	biceps torso musculature
5. Bench Press (8-12 reps):	triceps pectorals deltoids
6. Barbell Curl (8-12 reps):	biceps
7. Parallel Dips (8-12 reps):	triceps pectorals deltoids
8. Barbell Dead Lift (12-15 reps):	gluteals hamstrings lower back

Free Weight Workout
Exercise #1: Full Squat

Starting and Finishing Position

Mid-Range Position

Deep Squat Position

Free Weight Workout
Exercise #2: Chin-Ups

Starting and Finishing Position

Mid-Range Position

The Workout – Sample Workouts 151

Free Weight Workout
Exercise #3: Overhead Press

Starting and Finishing Position

Mid-Range Position

Free Weight Workout
Exercise #4: Bentover Row

Starting and Finishing Position

Mid-Range Position

Free Weight Workout
Exercise #5: Bench Press

Starting and Finishing Position

Mid-Range Position

Free Weight Workout
Exercise #6: Barbell Curl

Starting Position

Mid-Range Position

Finishing Position

Free Weight Workout
Exercise #7: Parallel Dips

Starting and Finishing Position

Mid-Range Position

Free Weight Workout
Exercise #8: Barbell Deadlift

Starting Position

Mid-Range Position

Finishing Position

IV. Cool Down: A Final Word

After reading this book, you are on to something monumental: The most meaningful exercise is accessible, doesn't take much time and can be virtually the same for everyone, the only difference being the level of intensity.

High-intensity strength training performed twice weekly is the best prescription for your body because it can provide the safest and most efficient workout. It stimulates results in muscle and bone strength, flexibility and cardio-respiratory conditioning, and provides plenty of rest in between workouts to allow those results. The principles discussed and exercises recommended here make complete physical fitness a matter of reasoned certainty – not haphazard guesswork.

Acknowledgements

Strength Of A Woman was written to present the truth about exercise and how it relates to women (which truth pertains equally to men). Completion was ultimately accomplished thanks to the guidance, patience, and love of Elanna, whose pictures on the cover and throughout the book taken "three babies later," illustrate the integrity, focus, and commitment from which this book was born.

Thanks also to Jim Waltzer for his hours of listening and editorial assistance, Kristine Eckenrode, whose photography captured our efforts and Todd Davidson who believed enough in the "truth" to get this book on the shelves.

More thanks to Chuck Bixby, Jeff Greenberg and Richard LaPlante who read and critiqued the manuscript. And to George Huston and Activewear Express who supplied the workout clothing. And finally to those who were there every step of the journey – Jesse, Juliette, Gabrielle, Liz, and Anne and the staff of Main Line Health and Fitness. And to my dad, Milton – I hope you would be proud of me.

Index

abdominal 49, 90, 110, 111, 125, 127, 144
abduction 74, 110, 111, 117
adduction 110, 111, 117
aerobics 2, 4-6, 14, 15, 39, 58, 65, 76, 79, 86
American College of Obstetrics and Gynecology 76
American College of Sports Medicine 4
anaerobic 4, 13, 18, 23, 25
arm cross 36, 38, 41, 110, 111, 122
arthritis 85, 86
assisted dip 110, 127, 141
assisted chin 110, 127, 139
athletes 58, 59, 61, 63, 64
barbell curl 29-31, 110, 147, 148, 154
barbell squat 103, 104, 110, 147, 148
bent-over row 16, 110, 147, 148, 152
bench press 35-38, 110, 147, 148, 153
bicep curl 110, 127, 138
bodybuilding 29, 51, 53, 55, 59
caloric intake 26, 46
cardio-respiratory system 97
cellulite 28, 86, 87
cervical extension 110, 127, 145

cervical spine 9, 92, 93, 147
chest press 110, 111, 123
childbirth 73, 78
chin-ups 33, 110, 147, 148, 150
circuit-type strength training 9, 12, 13, 15, 72
concentric 96
connective tissue 2, 7, 9, 46, 64, 69, 74, 79
Cooper, Kenneth H. 1, 14
deadlift 110, 147, 148, 156
degenerative change 93
dips 37, 110, 127
dumbbell fly 40, 41
eating/diet 10-12, 19, 21, 42, 49, 50, 56, 61, 68, 69, 90
estrogen 73, 79, 81, 85
explosive training 58, 60
flexibility 15, 25, 26, 28, 39, 42, 63, 70, 82
full range of motion 15-17, 28, 31-34, 54, 61
functional ability 27, 28, 49, 82
genetics 42, 47, 48, 51, 58
heart and lungs 1, 23, 65, 76
hip extension 74, 110, 111, 112, 127, 128
impact forces 8, 44, 75
indirect effect 88
joint stability 4

Index (continued)

joint stress 1, 6
Jones, Arthur 25, 29, 32
Journal of the American Medical Association 85
knee 8, 9, 20, 34, 59
lateral raise 110, 127, 136
leg curl 110, 111, 114, 115, 127, 130, 131
leg extension 34, 35, 45, 110, 111, 113, 127, 129
leg press 101, 110, 111, 116, 127, 132
lumbar extension 110, 111, 126
lumbar spine 90, 91, 147
MedX 20, 24, 31, 103, 104, 146
menopause 73, 79, 85
metabolic conditioning 25
metabolism 47, 50
muscular failure 25, 46, 99, 100
muscle fibers 6, 33, 42, 43
musculoskeletal system 24, 25, 39, 81, 97
Nautilus 29, 63, 66
nervous system 38, 39
osteoporosis 79, 81, 85, 91
overhead press 110, 127, 137, 147, 148, 151
overuse 7, 59
parallel dips 110, 147, 148, 155
preacher curl 30

pre-exhaustion 95, 101, 102, 105
pregnancy 75-79
pullover torso 17, 110, 111, 119, 127, 133
record keeping 95, 107
rehabilitation 88, 89, 92-94
rowing 21, 44, 59, 110, 111, 120, 127, 134
running 7, 10, 13, 22, 24
seated dip 110, 142
split workouts 59, 62
structural integrity 2, 7, 44, 46
subcutaneous fat 86
testosterone 51, 53, 55
torso arm 110, 111, 121, 127, 135
torso flexion 110, 111, 124, 127, 143
tricep extension 110, 127, 140
weight-bearing 43, 44
workout journal 106

Order Form

To order additional copies of
Strength Of A Woman
...The Truth About Training The Female Body

simply call toll free:
1-888-97WOMAN
Visa and MasterCard Accepted
OR
Send a check for $19.95
(plus $3.95 for shipping) to:

Main Line Publications
931 Haverford Road
Bryn Mawr, PA 19010

Please make check payable to:
Main Line Publications

CALL AND ORDER TODAY!
Thank You.

Strength Of A Woman
**A Revolutionary Approach
To Training The Female Body**
(Based on the book by Roger Schwab)

is available on VHS
Videocassette, produced by
NFL Films.
Price: $19.95 plus $3.95 Shipping

To order call toll free:
1-888-97WOMAN